Flying to the Sun

Britannia

Flying to the Sun

Quarter century of Britannia Airways, Europe's leading leisure airline.

GEOFFREY CUTHBERT

HODDER AND STOUGHTON
LONDON SYDNEY AUCKLAND TORONTO

The illustrations in this book have been selected from the Britannia Airways picture library, including work by Patrick Lichfield and Iain Dempster. While most illustrations are Britannia Airways copyright, acknowledgement and thanks are due to the following for further illustrations:
Waller Studios Ltd, Luton; Thomson Newspapers Ltd; MacDonald and Jane's; The Boeing Company, Seattle; Evening Post, Luton; World Press Features; Goodchilds Ltd, London WC2; British Aerospace; Theo Theodore, Luton; and members of Britannia Airways staff.

Book design by Stephen Raw

British Library Cataloguing in Publication Data

Cuthbert, Geoffrey
Flying to the sun: quarter century of Britannia Airways, Europe's leading leisure airline.
1. Britannia Airways – History
I. Title
387.7'065'41 HE9843.B6

ISBN 0 340 41020 5

First published in 1987

Typeset in Linotron Palatino by Rowland Phototypesetting Ltd, Bury St Edmunds, Suffolk
Printed and bound in Great Britain for Hodder and Stoughton Educational, a division of Hodder and Stoughton Ltd, Dunton Green, Sevenoaks, Kent, by A. Wheaton & Co. Ltd, Exeter, Devon.

Contents

FOREWORD

by the Countess Mountbatten of Burma

In 1984, I was very pleased to accept an invitation, together with my two youngest sons, Philip and Timothy, to a ceremony at Britannia Airways when we named the first of Britannia's Boeing 767 fleet after my father. Since that day, G-BKPW *The Earl Mountbatten of Burma* has flown many hundreds of thousands of passengers to holidays in the sun.

I am, therefore, pleased to have been invited to contribute the foreword to this history of Britannia Airways which, in 1987 is celebrating its twenty-fifth anniversary. This is a story of an airline that set out from the start with a determination that it should adopt high standards in every aspect of its operations. It is a chronicle of a period in which charter airlines have developed from underfunded organisations operating second rate, second hand equipment into solid, top quality companies operating the most cost-effective and efficient flights in Europe, carrying many millions of passengers on some of the most modern aircraft flying. Britannia has played a major part in bringing about this change and in introducing low-cost travel to many millions of Britons.

BOEING 767

** WELCOME **
ABOARD

Preparing for take-off

CHAPTER ONE

The loudest roar in London on Saturday, May 5, 1962, erupted like vocal lava through the crater above Wembley Stadium. The massed supporters of Tottenham Hotspur Football Club were hailing their victorious captain, Danny Blanchflower, as he received the FA Cup from the Queen.

Eight hours earlier and 23 miles to the north, there had been a roar of a different kind. At 9.20am, the four 2,200 horsepower piston engines of a Lockheed Constellation, the world's first pressurised passenger aircraft, began to splutter into life. On the runway of little-used Luton Airport, Captain Peter Edwards was about to take Golf-Alpha Romeo Victor Papa on a positioning sector to Manchester's Ringway Airport which, by coincidence, is only a few miles from the hometown of Burnley, the opponents of Spurs in that Wembley final.

It was one hour 50 minutes later, at 11.10am, that Captain Edwards rolled Victor Papa along Manchester's runway for his second take-off of the day, and so marked a milestone event in aviation just as surely as Blanchflower and his team that afternoon secured the name of Tottenham Hotspur in the record books of Association Football.

For that air journey – to Perpignan in south-west France and on to Palma, Majorca – was the inaugural flight of an enterprise, today known as Britannia Airways, which, well before it celebrated its quarter century in 1987, had grown into the biggest leisure airline in Europe.

It was just before midnight on that rainy May Saturday when a wearying Captain Edwards returned to England with the Constellation, taxi-ing into the unhurried calm of Luton Airport. In stark contrast, on a summer Saturday 25 years later, modern, bustling Luton International would be just one of several UK airports handling as many as 178 flights for Britannia carrying around 25,000 holidaymakers, many of them in the wide-bodied luxury of Boeing 767 aircraft seating 273 passengers compared with just 82 in that first Constellation.

In the age of the mass package holiday, Britannia Airways and its rival airlines fly ten million Britons a year to sun-kissed holiday destinations such as Spain, Italy, Yugoslavia, Greece and further afield. No relation to the holiday scene in 1961, the year a meeting took place in a windowless cubicle of an office in London's Piccadilly which was to become not just the pathfinder for the inaugural flight the following year,

Captain Peter Edwards, at the top of the steps, who piloted the historic first flight to Palma on May 5, 1962.

but also arguably the catalyst for what is now the highly-specialised United Kingdom inclusive tour industry in which 1987 expenditure on holidays by air was forecast to reach nearly £3 billion.

Despite the people's having been told by the then Prime Minister, Harold Macmillan, that they "had never had it so good", Blackpool and other traditional seaside resorts were, in 1961, still the favourite holiday destinations for the vast majority of Britons. Benidorm was not even marked on most maps of Spain, and the Mediterranean coastal province of Alicante – to whose airport Britannia now fly more than a thousand holidaymakers a day in season – acknowledged wine, fruit, fish and fabrics among its industries . . . but not tourism.

Mention charter airlines to the man-in-the-street at that time and his impression of them was likely to be of cowboy operators existing on the proverbial wing and a prayer. The reason for this was not hard to discover. In 1949, the intransigence of the Russians had brought Western Europe to its closest brush with World War Three. Berlin had been peremptorily cut off from supplies, causing the West to mount the Berlin Airlift for which every available aircraft was mobilised.

Afterwards, several of the men who had taken part became ambitious to set up airlines of their own, most of them on a shoestring budget. They bought the aircraft for next to nothing and, without a sustaining capital base, many soon became unreliable operators. Their dubious enterprises unfortunately gave an unacceptable – and generally unwarranted – public image to the whole of aviation chartering.

A man worried about the quality of flying he could then obtain was Captain Ted Langton who ran one of the first and leading inclusive tour operations, Universal Sky Tours. At the end of the fifties, he had become so anxious about the effect this could have on his tour business that he commissioned a study to discover whether it would be possible to form a reputable airline, in association with his tour operation, to ensure he had the quality he needed to attract more customers.

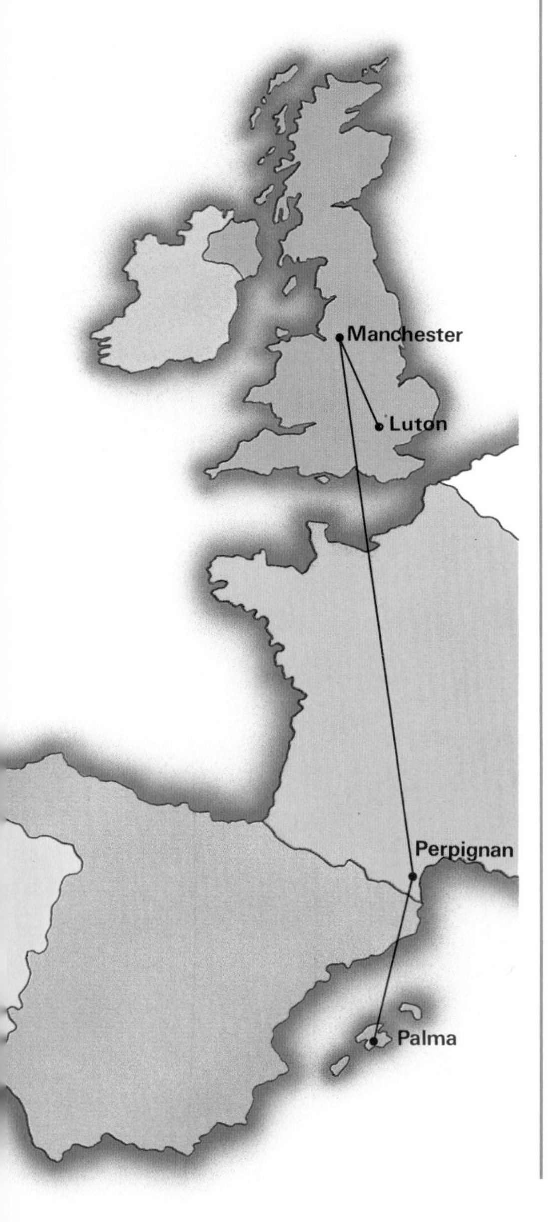

The pioneering flight path. Constellation G-ARVP made Euravia's maiden flight from Luton to Manchester for positioning to take holidaymakers to Palma via Perpignan in France.

Langton had originally refined his concept in a land-based, UK setting. The idea for his system-designed holidays began in a Liverpool pub when a coach operator was bemoaning lack of business, and Langton asked him how much he would charge to put a coach continuously on the road throughout the summer. Armed with the low quotation he received, Langton toured Devon and Cornwall looking for hotel and boarding-house keepers who had difficulty filling their rooms. Selecting the most desperate, he offered a deal to give them continuous occupancy throughout the season.

Thus was born the 'hot bed' routine whereby – on what tour operators today call 'back-to-back' packages – coaches from the north ferried holidaymakers to the south-west to fill the beds left by departing customers whom they then coached back home.

Langton soon decided to apply the same technique overseas knowing it was more critical for hoteliers than airline operators to ensure they had guaranteed pre-bookings. It was on this vulnerability that Langton played his ace card. He would go round the world looking at hotels, with the ability quickly to sniff out those having problems.

As one of his later associates recalls: "The technique was to say he would take all the hotelier's beds for the season, and then screw, screw and screw again so that he could get an acceptable price. If the man could not be screwed, he would abandon the hotel and find another whose owner could be screwed. It worked well with hotel owners and coach operators, but what Langton fell foul of was the airlines because, adopting the same technique with them, he inevitably got mixed up with the 'cowboy' operators.

"Though he never philosophised about it or explained it, it seemed quite clear that Langton had discovered something wrong with his technique because in dealing with the cowboys something always went wrong. At its worst, he saw companies go bust with passengers ending up stranded at a resort. On the other hand, he did not want to pay the seat prices demanded by State airlines".

So it was that scenario which convinced Ted Langton that the only answer was to start his own airline. It was not his style, however, to come out in the open and say so, though he might drop the thought in conversation to see what the reaction was.

It was sheer coincidence that at precisely the same time, John Ernest Derek Williams, then a London aviation consultant, had evolved the concept of a vertically integrated system design of travel to create a holiday package. As far as he is aware, he wrote the first article to be published advocating the policy.

"I was full of my ideas, but I did not know that Langton, of whom I had never heard, had been working along these lines for some years in the charabanc business," Williams admits.

Equally unknown to Langton, 'Jed' Williams had been introduced to an extrovert aircraft dealer called Len Orman by Itzhak Shander who, nearly 20 years later, became president of El Al. Within two months of that meeting, Orman came to Jed Williams' office asking whether he would help him sell three Constellation aircraft which El Al no longer required. The reward would certainly be worth the effort – half the commission El Al were to pay Orman.

It was only then that Jed Williams learned the name of the potential purchaser: Captain Ted Langton. Though the name meant nothing to Williams, he was soon to meet the full blast of the colourful personality behind it.

Langton was a character who showed great personal creativity and imagination – not least being his adoption of the rank of 'Captain' – and he led something of a Jekyll and Hyde existence in both his business and private life.

It was Langton who had the airless, windowless office in Piccadilly where he would spend around nine hours a day, six days a week, keeping his fingers on all items connected with Universal Sky Tours. He was everything from the stamp licker to the price fixer. But around 8pm each day he would leave for another of his business interests, the Blue Angel night club, where Danny La Rue started his career as a female drag artist.

Not only had Jed Williams never heard of Langton, equally he had never sold an aircraft in his life. He could not have had a more difficult or taciturn first customer.

Having negotiated a passageway between Universal Sky Tours' Piccadilly shop and the administrative office above it, Len Orman and Jed Williams found Langton's sparse office which itself formed part of the passage.

The two potential aircraft sellers sat there uncomfortably as office workers distractingly passed to and fro and Ted Langton read his mail. There was complete disinterest both in the visitors and their mission. As Jed Williams reported: "He did not want to buy aeroplanes, did not like aeroplanes, and showed no interest in making my acquaintance."

Williams, the then rookie salesman, acknowledges that Len Orman was made of sterner stuff. Orman grudgingly got the admission from Langton that, just possibly, he could be in the market for aeroplanes for a new Spanish airline he was starting with Spanish associates, to be called Hispair. Not only had Williams been unaware that the vertically integrated holiday concept had been exercising Langton's mind, but also of the background to how Spain fitted into the picture.

As a result of that spark of interest, however, Ted Langton and Jed Williams flew to Tel Aviv and met Williams' old boss, General Ben Arzi, in his office as chairman of the board of El Al. Not unexpectedly, Langton

Ted Langton (right), *the tour operator who wanted to start his own airline, with Jed Williams who was given the challenge of getting it off the ground.*

taciturnly showed no interest in buying the General's Constellations and it became obvious to Williams that no deal was to be struck. He tells, however, of the surprising events that followed:

"I went on my own to Israel Aircraft Industries, also government owned, and suggested that they sell the aircraft to Langton, fully overhauled and converted to his high density seating, in a package which would include ongoing engine and component overhaul business for them. Following a day of discussions and, we can be sure, some tough talking behind the scenes between IAI and El Al, Langton and I met the managing director of IAI the next evening in the bar of the Dan hotel. As usual Langton said nothing.

"We got down to £90,000 for three Constellations, fully overhauled in 82 seater configuration, plus a consignment of spare engines and parts which would remain the property of IAI. The overhauls alone were worth more than £60,000.

"I stared helplessly at Langton. He had to say something. I was finished. Langton fished a scrap of paper out of his pocket and wrote some numbers on it. He stared at them for a couple of minutes and then read them aloud slowly. They were the dates at which he would make progress payments. He had bought!

"On the flight back to London, Langton talked to me at length for the first time. Aviation legislation had been transformed in 1960. To carry paying passengers one required an Air Operator's Certificate from the newly created Director of Aviation Safety – a man who had enormous personal powers including the right to withdraw a certificate in the middle of the night without warning – and a licence for the particular service from a new Air Transport Licensing Board. They issued licences having regard to the public need, the diversion of traffic from existing licence holders and fitness of the operator (except in matters of safety), particularly financial fitness.

"Langton saw this legislation simply as a bag of tricks designed to entrench British European Airways – the forerunner of British Airways – and put people like himself out of business. I disagreed. We argued.

"He saw Spain as the big growth area, and he would by-pass the whole system with his own Spanish airline to which it would be politically impossible for the British to refuse traffic rights."

Universal Sky Tours — and Euravia — began life in a small office in London's Piccadilly. It is still a travel shop today, though under totally different ownership. Jed Williams' first office was behind the half-moon glass frontage on the first floor.

Now Williams realised what was in Langton's mind – the vertical integration of the components of the package holiday system.

"You will have to go to Madrid to see about getting these aircraft accepted," Langton instructed Williams, who recalls: "I accepted, as a consultant, and pointed out that my meter was now ticking to his account. He grunted acquiescence."

But a couple of weeks later came the shattering denouement.

"After boarding a Madrid flight at Heathrow, I was astonished to see John Bruno, Langton's right hand man, sitting breathlessly beside me."

"Just made it," he said, "Captain Langton sent me to tell you that he wants your mission to fail. He doesn't want a Spanish airline now."

Jed Williams responded decisively: "Doesn't he realise that he has bought the aircraft and cannot now back out?"

"That's not it," retorted Bruno. "Now he wants a British airline and he wants you to be

▲

One of the airline's first Constellation aircraft in flight, showing the Euravia livery.

managing director."

And so it was those fourteen words which led to what has now become Europe's leading holiday airline, Britannia Airways.

But, if he accepted, Jed Williams was under no illusion of what he was taking on. He had already experienced the traumas of life with his new boss and, from experience both on the flight deck and in his consultancy, he knew the caprices of the aircraft fleet he was inheriting. Those 049 type Constellations had BA-3 Curtiss Wright engines notorious for their oil leaks, the fuel tanks leaked fuel, and the pressurisation system leaked air. Maybe they were cheap at £30,000 each, but the cost of maintaining those aircraft could be open-ended.

And there was no question that capital was going to be tight. Jed Williams soon discovered that this was not Langton's first dabble in the world of aviation. His links with charter airlines had a chequered history, some of them having failed financially and others on grounds of safety.

But to ensure the standards he believed to be the minimum, the start up capital should certainly not be less than £25,000, though he would demand £50,000. This would all be in the form of fully paid share capital, together with the extra security that Universal Sky Tours would give the airline through cast iron aircraft leases and charter contracts.

When he walked into Langton's office to put his demands, Williams found his boss closeted with the company's auditors whose senior partner was forcefully condemning the airline enterprise as hairbrained. The blunt truth was that, professionally, he knew Langton could not afford the expansion.

Even so, Langton's fixed glare masking a false bravado, he announced to Williams: "The share capital will be £25,000." The beginnings of protest were smothered by the assertion: "You can put up £5,000 if you want to."

Williams' understanding of that was that for £5,000 he could have a fifth of a £25,000 company or a sixth of a £30,000 business.

"If you put up twenty, I'll put up five," was Williams' immediate response.

Equally dogmatically, Langton proclaimed that the name of the airline was to be Euravia. It was relevant in contemporary Britain because of the development of the European Common Market, allied to the fact that, apparently, in Ted Langton's mind there was the notion that if it proved impossible to fly under the Union Jack, then the operation could be switched to Holland.

Jed Williams, however, had to concentrate all his attention on the close challenge of the present rather than the long stop that might be needed later in the innings. The immediate need was to recruit the people to get the fledgling airline off the ground.

There were grim precedents for failure, too historically close for comfort. The reason Ted Langton was now involved with his own airline was that the two charter companies he had mostly been using, Falcon Airways and Air Safaris, had ceased operations. What was needed by Euravia was instant experience.

Williams had to reach out no further than his own consultancy for the man to take the righthand seat on the Euravia corporate flight deck. Captain John ('Jackie') Harrington had served with Imperial Airways, its successor British Overseas Airways Corporation, and the Bristol Aeroplane Company.

A few months earlier, after retiring from Bristol, he had joined the board of consultants J. E. D. Williams Ltd. Here was the ready-made man to infuse operational experience. Third man on the list of directors was to be an outside accountant nominated by Langton, but in the event Langton's auditors provided one of their staff to become company secretary.

So it was that official documents show Euravia (London) Limited to have been registered on December 1, 1961, with J. E. D. Williams as managing director, Captain J. C. Harrington as a director, and with the Universal Sky Tours representative being P. J. Ward who was also company secretary.

It was reported at the time that the airline was backed by large travel interests and would be based at an airport as yet undecided but "in the London area".

Who, then, was this man who created an airline which, re-named Britannia Airways, was to become, by any financial yardstick, the most successful air transport venture Europe has seen? Nearly a quarter of a century later, sitting in his garden amid terracotta pots cascading with the myriad coloured plants sustained by an Italian summer, Jed Williams surveyed the silent, verdant Apennines on the horizon. Behind him stood his more recent creation – the transformation of a centuries-old derelict Tuscan farmhouse into a luxurious villa, the heart of an estate where he now grows olives, tends sheep, and carries out afforestation on the sheer, commanding hillside which provides him with an immense backdrop of undisturbed privacy.

The scene is as far removed from England, apart from the ever-present packets of Senior Service and the gentle aroma of Fortnum and Mason's finest Darjeeling, as is the solitude from the incessant bustle of aviation activity. Yet aircraft were Williams' whole life for three decades.

His first glimpse of the compulsive world of aviation came in wartime Liverpool, the city of his birth in 1923, when he joined the University Air Squadron. It was barely a sighting, for by the tender age of 19 he was in the Royal Air Force serving as a navigator in Egypt. His activity varied from escorting convoys towards the strategic island of Malta, to striking shipping off the Greek islands.

It was during the invasion of Sicily and Italy that he learned the art of multi-discipline line activity, for as well as being a navigator he also had to carry out the roles of rear gunner, wireless operator and reconnaissance photographer, together with operating an Aldis lamp to communicate with the Royal Navy.

The multifarious tasks of wartime navigation did not disillusion him against pursuing the profession in peacetime. Achieving a civil aircraft navigator's licence was his career passport for the next ten years which were spent overseas as chief navigator for Aerolineas Argentinas and El Al. Creativity opened up for Jed Williams when the Israeli airline appointed him manager of operational development where he cultivated the art of flying aircraft more economically through greater navigational precision. Later, he became technical adviser to El Al's chairman.

It was in 1959 that he returned to London to start his consultancy – and that was the fateful decision which put him in the right place at the right time to become the catalyst for the formation of Euravia.

Now, as he sits in the tranquillity of Tuscany with his Dutch-born wife Marianne – who was chief stewardess on that first Euravia flight – Jed Williams readily acknowledges the significance of Ted Langton in the history of the travel business.

He is unequivocal in his view:

"I quite seriously maintain Langton was the greatest man in travel since Thomas Cook – and if you look at it in many ways, his contribution was the greater."

Cook, he recalls, was the first to charter a train as a 'middle man', but he moved away from the chartering concept. By contrast it was Ted Langton's epitaph that he developed the system design formula for holidays. This consisted of two weeks on a beach at a certain price based on 100 per cent occupancy of aeroplane seats and hotel beds.

Jed Williams vividly recalls that journey to Israel with Langton: "I was a great talker and he was a good listener. Five years later, in retrospect, it became clear to me that Ted Langton started a British airline not only because he took to my ideas and was impressed that I was not a cowboy, because of the way I was treated by the people in El Al from the chairman downwards, but that he believed here was someone who had three qualifications from his point of view – an outlook coinciding with his own on the kind of airline he should have; a technical standing and professionalism; and a clear vision of how an airline should be managed."

There was no doubt that his El Al experiences were invaluable background for Jed Williams' new challenge. One of his jobs in Israel was to be a 'backroom boy' detached from routine activity but given the role of a one-man think tank to analyse the significance of the coming jet age, with aircraft such as the Boeing 707 and the Douglas DC-8. It gave him an unusual grasp of the economics of the airline industry, and this knowledge was enhanced with commissions during his later consultancy role – all input which a line manager would find it impossible to acquire because of his day-to-day operational role.

Even so, Jed Williams ruefully admits: "I had been in state airlines, so I had no background in the kind of business where you have to worry about how you pay the wages on Friday. It was a totally new experience for me."

With five months to go before the roar of that first flight, there was certainly no time to allow for the luxury of a learning curve. It was a straight line to ensuring planned take-off.

Jed Williams, with his wife Marianne, who was chief stewardess on the first Euravia flight, at their farmhouse home overlooking the Apennine hills in Italy.

CHAPTER TWO

Chocks away

Companies House recorded the registration of the new airline on December 1, 1961. What it did not reveal was that on the day of registration, the business did not have a single aircraft to fly. Even had it done so, there would have been no-one to pilot it, no engineers to service it, and no home airport to take-off from. Just one other little local difficulty – it did not even have a licence to fly!

Nevertheless, on the registration day, Williams and Harrington started work, faced with a forbidding agenda listing hundreds of items. The four critical ones were to build up the management base from just two, to find a home airport, to secure route licences, and to achieve their air operator's certificate.

As Jed Williams later recalled: "I was determined that the people I thought to be key in operating these difficult aircraft (the three Lockheed Constellations) – the chief pilot and chief engineer – should be people whom I knew and trusted and who had known and distrusted these aircraft in El Al."

One of those 'distrusters' was Derek Harold Davison. Then 39, he was a training captain with El Al – and unknown to him, his already impressive aviation career, spanning twenty years, was to be eclipsed by the imprint he stamped on the succeeding decades of an embryonic airline.

By then, Derek Davison had flown for two airlines other than El Al – BOAC and Pakistan International. After leaving the Royal Air Force in 1947, his flight-deck experience had been a reflection of the immediate post-war civil aviation scene – Tudors, Yorks, Argonauts, Constellations, Britannias and Comets.

One day, a letter arrived in Tel Aviv for him from his former El Al colleague, Jed Williams. The two of them had been quite close – in fact, they used to take each other's children back to boarding-school in England. He was being offered the job of chief pilot of Euravia.

"I was the last overseas contract pilot left with El Al and was enjoying rates of compensation considerably better than those paid to the locals," Derek Davison recalls.

"I had done three years in Israel, following four years in Pakistan which I hadn't enjoyed because of the climate. I had got on very well with the Israelis, but it was attractive to me to return to the UK. Also I recognised Jed's capabilities. I had every confidence that anything he was involved in would be a success, and the job of chief pilot at the outset of a new company certainly attracted me. El Al were very amenable and allowed me to go."

Perhaps Jed Williams was, at heart, not all that confident he had the bait to capture his fish.

"There he was working for a state airline, and there was me coming and saying: 'Look, I've got this crazy character Ted Langton to work for. Come and be chief pilot.'"

Derek Davison was enough of a realist to appreciate that it was an era of survival of only the fittest.

"I knew nothing of the whole of the background in the UK. I only knew what I had read about charter companies in Flight magazine and other sources.

"I think the philosophy associated with an airline in the early days must be geared to survival rather than to the future. It was certainly very much touch and go whether we survived or not in our early days. One or two of my friends had left BOAC and gone into charter airlines and none of them had done terribly well out of it." Davison was to discover the truth of this when he began recruiting staff for the new airline and found out the number of times pilots had changed their jobs.

Some recruiting had, of course, already taken place to fill various positions.

From another distinguished airline, Pan American, came Sid Finnegan as chief engineer.

These two, together with Marianne Allen as chief stewardess, were to join a small team which had been assembled by Jackie Harrington – Ernest Hessey as operations manager, Captain Roy McDougall as deputy chief pilot, and Mike Forster as chief flight engineer.

The distinction of being the first staff recruit to the airline belongs to Roy McDougall who could put forward a fascinating career background. He joined the RAF in 1939, when he was only 18, following his education in Rhodesia – now Zimbabwe – where he was born. His 5½ years in the RAF, during which he was awarded the Distinguished Flying Cross, encompassed two bombing tours in Germany and Burma. This included two 'firsts' – he led the first RAF daylight raid against the Japanese and he took part in the longest raid of World War Two, from India to Bangkok.

On leaving the service, he was seconded to BOAC and commanded Lancastrians, an airliner conversion of the famous Lancaster bomber. He was later involved in the earliest stages of post-war German civil aviation when, as chief pilot/operations manager for LTU, he not only helped establish the airline but also recruited and trained its pilots. He moved on to the company known today as Condor, the Lufthansa charter subsidiary. The then Captain McDougall earned the nickname 'McSchnell' from the Germans because of his ability to achieve fast turnrounds of aircraft.

Before he joined Euravia he had become a freelance pilot, and one of his most demanding jobs was to evacuate people from the Belgian Congo when the Hermes aircraft being used carried loads far exceeding accepted levels.

But some of his most vivid memories are still those early days of Euravia.

At the beginning of the sixties, the employment climate was not good for pilots, no matter how experienced or proficient they were. Too many fledgling airlines were going to the wall. In those lean years, Roy McDougall had developed an idea for a flight-deck manual specifically for use by charter airlines. The normal manuals used by schedule airlines were not appropriate for the smaller independents. Not only did they need to have facts on the remote airfields, but McDougall believed that safety heights should be included on the radio navigational charts rather than, at that time, only on topographical maps. After being shown the door by one aviation map supplier, he explained his thinking to Swissair who greeted it with enthusiasm. The next stop was the Jeppesen organisation in Denver, Colorado, leaders in aviation manuals. They warmly greeted the idea and said they would produce air navigation charts incorporating the McDougall suggestions.

And so it was that Roy McDougall found himself making several visits to those cramped offices of Universal Sky Tours and Euravia in Piccadilly. Though he was trying to sell them the new charter manual, Jackie Harrington, whom

Derek Davison, in his early days as Euravia's chief pilot, captaining a Constellation. He joined the airline after flying for BOAC, Pakistan International and El Al.

Luton Airport's first terminal building, with, on the right, the new extension built especially for Euravia.

Below *The first Constellations lined up on the apron at Luton.*

McDougall had known in his BOAC days, got the impression the pilot-turned-itinerant-salesman was asking for a job. That wasn't the case, but on the third visit by McDougall, Harrington asked him whether he would like the post of deputy chief pilot.

"Well," replied McDougall, "are you going to buy my manuals?" It turned out to be a two-way deal: Euravia bought the manuals – and employed their inventor.

His instant task was to interview potential flight crew for Euravia. Each day he would travel to Green Park tube station and enter the little office nearby. You can still see the office today – the building even houses a travel agency. At 93 Piccadilly, it is easily identified by the half-moon of glass above the frontage. It was behind that architectural oddity that Euravia saw the light of day. To reach the Euravia room upstairs, McDougall would pass the ground floor section from which Universal Sky Tours sold their holidays. Invariably, there was a little man standing behind a desk with ash cascading down the front of his suit. Intrigued, Roy McDougall inquired from Jed Williams and Jackie Harrington who the curious chap was downstairs.

"You'd better come down and meet him," Williams replied. "He's your boss." It was Ted Langton.

Williams spent his days in Piccadilly constantly trying to drum up business for the airline. It was obvious, however, that not only were the temporary offices too small for the increasing numbers of staff, but there would be a distinct advantage in being at the sharp end of the airline's future operations. But where was that home base to be?

Today, London Gatwick is the world's third biggest international airport handling 15 million passengers a year. At the beginning of the sixties, it was still very much at the start of its expansion years, and the airport commandant was witnessing charter airlines given birth and then dying almost with the rapidity of the common butterfly. This airline life-cycle certainly coloured the response of the commandant when Jed Williams approached him with the idea of Euravia's making Gatwick its base.

They could, he said grudgingly, fly from his domain but they would not be allowed any facilities, and he insisted that their aircraft handling and maintenance, and passenger handling and catering, must be undertaken by the established operators there.

This was not to Williams' taste and when he related his reception to Ted Langton, he responded: "You'll be visiting Luton, I suppose?"

It was that remark which began a long and harmonious relationship between the airline and a municipal corporation whose town was until then noted for two industries – hatmaking and Vauxhall, the British subsidiary of General Motors.

So from the Surrey-Sussex borders of a then rather inaccessible Gatwick, Jed Williams, accompanied by Jackie Harrington, travelled to the other side of London, 20 odd miles up the then recently constructed M1 – the first of Britain's motorways – to an airport perched on a plateau above the town of Luton.

It happened that the airport commandant, Peter Rushton, was on holiday, so they were met by Bob Easterbrook, then the air traffic control manager, but some years later the airport's director.

"The story these two characters gave me – and obviously I was a lot more naive then than I am now – was that they were consultants for a potential airline and they were evaluating a number of possible sites in southern England to establish it. I showed them round and they said the facilities were hopelessly inadequate."

One inadequacy which embarrassed Easterbrook was that he usually took sandwiches from home for his lunch as there were no catering facilities at the airport. But he thought the two visitors meant business, so he rang the managing director of an aero engine company, one of the airport's tenants, and bulldozed him into giving Williams and Harrington lunch. A few weeks later, the bill came in – all of 7s.6d. (37½ pence) each – and the airport accountant strongly challenged the exhorbitant price.

Even if they weren't unduly impressed by the lunch, the duo obviously thought Luton was worth a second visit when they found Peter Rushton enthusiastically ready to show them not only a sound runway aided by reasonable navigation facilities, but also, importantly, a new empty hangar. That was the good news for the arrival of Euravia's Constellations; the bad news was that the puny terminal building would not be able to handle a single Constellation passenger load.

Only three days after Christmas, however, Jed Williams and Jackie Harrington were meeting Luton's mayor, town clerk and a clutch of councillors and officials. It did not take them long to propose building a temporary terminal which would be ready to receive 250 passengers within four months.

"We shall have the aircraft to make something of your airport," is what Jed Williams told them in a mixture of ebullience and bravado. At the time, this easily forgotten airport, which was established before World War Two as a simple grass runway airfield, had only one airline using it – Autair (forerunner of the ill-fated Court Line) which was operating a service to Blackpool.

Jed Williams (left) meets Luton Airport's commandant Peter Rushton who was enthusiastic to have Euravia as a potentially important operator.

Right *Luton's Mayor, George Llewellyn Matthews, on board a Euravia Constellation. He and his civic team did not take long to endorse Rushton's enthusiasm.*

"We took to the Luton people and they took to us. They had a nice long runway and a lovely big empty hangar – and enthusiasm. I knew I could sell Luton to Ted Langton because of that new M1 Motorway which made it nearer to London than Gatwick," Williams says.

That was critical because, in those days, charter travel began, for most people, in Central London. Euravia had established a town terminal in an old Avon tyre works near Euston station from where passengers were bussed to the airport. That was particularly convenient for holidaymakers travelling on the overnight trains from Scotland and the north.

If the financial deal with the then Town Clerk of Luton, Don Harvey, and his airport committee was an ace for Euravia, the trump card deftly played by Jed Williams was an astute arrangement that the airport would not have a duty free shop. "That particular perk was to be ours – and we exploited it," he admits.

So much so that today, even with duty free shops now at the airport, Britannia claims to be the biggest airline purveyor of duty free goods in the world, with £20 million of yearly sales. It is an achievement well recognised by its rivals – in 1985 Britannia was named In-Flight Tax Free Operator of the Year in the first international tax and duty free marketing awards.

There is no doubt that Euravia, later Britannia, was the airline cartographer responsible for drawing Luton on to the world airport map. In fact, its main challenger in bringing Luton into the consciousness of the public at large was a gawky young Cockney girl called Lorraine Chase who, many years later, captivated television viewers with the phrase "Nice 'ere, innit?" in a commercial with the airport as a backdrop.

In 1986, Luton had a throughput of 1.8 million passengers a year – of those Britannia carried around one million – and an average of 76 aircraft movements every day, though with a concentration on the summer months.

From the earliest days, duty free sales were an important aspect of the airline's activity. The growth of this business through the years culminated in the 1985 In-Flight Tax Free Operator of the Year award being won by Britannia Airways. In the picture Jack Moss, centre, the airline's in-flight services manager, receives the award with Dina Shaw, sales co-ordinator.

CHAPTER THREE

Lift-off

So now Euravia could contemplate the arrival of a chief pilot – El Al agreed to release Derek Davison for April 1 – three Constellations, and a home base from which to fly them. All they lacked were any routes on which to fly – and one or two minor corporate inadequacies such as no accounts department (which really, perhaps, did not matter because they did not have a sales department to nourish the bottom line).

So the next hurdle, in what had become a veritable decathlon of activity to get the airline off the ground, was to secure the rights for charter services from Britain's Air Transport Licensing Board, then under the chairmanship of Professor Daniel Jack.

The routes applied for were certainly varied. The records at the Kingsway, London, headquarters of the Civil Aviation Authority, successor to the ATLB, show that Euravia (London) Ltd, were applying for a licence in conjunction with Seamarks Bros Ltd (Airtours) of Luton "for the carriage of inclusive tour passengers between Luton and Palma, the licence to be in effect from 26 May to 29 September, 1962. The service would be operated at a frequency of one flight weekly in each direction on Fridays or Sundays with Constellation aircraft. The tariff to be from £53.11s.0d. to £72.19s.6d." This was granted subject to there only being one flight fortnightly instead of weekly. But another similar application from Luton to Perpignan was approved on a weekly basis.

The Board decided that a January day in 1962 would be set aside for the first hearing, the morning to be devoted to a public airing of Euravia's case on the need for their services and the objections to them, and the afternoon to be a private session on the airline's fitness to undertake the flights.

Jed Williams fought his own case and called just one witness, John Bruno, who had been the aerial messenger giving Williams the first news of Ted Langton's original decision to form a British airline.

This is how Williams recalls the hearing:

"The whole thing was silly and the debate on a low intellectual level. It was silly for three reasons. Firstly, we would not divert traffic from scheduled services, we would stimulate it, but the government and the Board would not entirely accept this argument for another three years or so. Secondly, the question of diversion of traffic from one charter airline to another was really an issue between tour organisers, not the airlines they happened to have contracted that year. Thirdly, everybody present knew that if Langton wanted to fly to Spain, nobody in Britain could, and nobody in Spain would, stop him from chartering a Spanish airline. One objector said he would not mind because the British public did not like flying by Spanish charter airlines. I wondered whose side he was on.

"The afternoon session was very different. I had, of course, given the Board, in advance, documentation with lots of appendices which purported to show that our operation would be viable, our cash adequate, our fleet ideal for our purpose, and that we in Euravia were splendid chaps at running airlines especially with the vast resources of Universal Sky Tours behind us. This time Jackie Harrington, the company secretary and I occupied the centre of the front row in the large empty hall. The Board outnumbered us more than two to one.

"The questioning started, courteous and deadly efficient. Almost immediately the accountant rushed to the loo and did not return, a consequence apparently of the deplorable pub lunch we had shared. Jackie sat cool, casual, strong and silent, looking just the chap to start an airline on £25,000. The trouble of course was the complete absence of any hard facts about those vast resources of Universal Sky Tours. The man they wanted before them, would always want and never get, was of course Langton.

"The claim that our fleet was ideal for our purpose was not entirely risible. At £30,000 per aircraft we could afford to keep our aeroplanes on the ground much of the time if necessary. It was a telling point at a curious moment in aviation history. The rights to international scheduled air services (almost all international air services at that time) were agreed between the governments concerned, and their nominated flag carriers had to offer identical fare structures. Since the airlines could not compete with each other on price, they were all obliged to buy jets as quickly as they appeared. Most of the world's pre-Boeing 707 fleet came on the market within three years. Charter airlines sprang up everywhere and disappeared as quickly. Established charter airlines were in trouble because they had paid too much for equipment suddenly obsolete.

"We got about 80 per cent of the licences we sought. Langton hid his relief by berating Bruno and me about the missing 20 per cent. In my opinion, against the background of those times, the Board would have been entirely justified in rejecting us entirely. That they did not is a tribute to the courage and insight of the members of the board, distinguished old gentlemen without any knowledge of aviation between them."

There were more applications the following month, but now existing operators were beginning to take note of this unknown airline called Euravia. When it applied for a route from London Gatwick to Palma and Barcelona there were objections from British European Airways, British United Airways (later absorbed into British Caledonian), Cunard Eagle, and even the puny East Anglian Flying Services of Southend. Nevertheless, the request was granted subject to the flights leaving from Luton rather than Gatwick.

By the time March arrived, there were some applications for longer, more exotic destinations including Casablanca – with a night stop in Tenerife – Tangier and Venice.

And there were early signs of Euravia's forward ambitions. In the next month or two, they had already submitted 34 applications for summer routes the following year. The broadening of UK departure points was shown by requests to fly from Glasgow, Belfast, Luton, Liverpool, Manchester and Cardiff to destinations including Palma, Valencia, Tarragona, Ibiza, Perpignan, Nice, Genoa, Alicante, Malaga, Tangier, Gerona, Barcelona and Tenerife.

Though Euravia still needed an Air Operator's Certificate, at least they could now offer routes to potential tour operator clients. But the biggest disappointment was with the chief shareholder. The level of bookings from Ted Langton's Universal Sky Tours indicated an ominous excess of supply over demand both in the licences awarded by the Air Transport Licensing Board and in the number of aircraft they were about to accept. There was not enough business even for two of the three Constellations.

With the climate of opinion surrounding charter operators at that time, it is not surprising that the whispering campaign had already encompassed Euravia. There were many tour operators who were ready to bet the airline would not get off the ground – and they were certainly not willing to risk their holidaymaker clients being stranded on a windswept Bedfordshire plateau rather than enjoying themselves on a Mediterranean beach.

Langton might have been monosyllabic – "that bloody airline of yours" is the phrase he frequently used to Jed Williams – but it was, after all, his money in the airline. After grudgingly admitting at the last minute that he only needed two aircraft, he came up with what proved to be a telling lead.

"There's a fellow in Birmingham who hasn't chartered his summer programme," he revealed to Williams, who immediately rushed to the Midlands to see the prospect. As a result, Williams came back armed with a whole summer programme to fill one of the Constellations. Not only that, the rate he negotiated was ten per cent higher than Langton was paying for his charters.

"It was a pleasure to tell him so," recalls Jed Williams. This Birmingham coup became the starting pistol for take-off.

There was need now to concentrate the corporate mind on securing that Air Operator's Certificate without which Euravia could not start their aircraft flying or cash flowing. It had to be won from the Directorate of Aviation Safety and to do so an airline must satisfy their officials on its operational performance and facilities – that it has the resources, equipment, skills and standards to fly passengers safely. This includes the preparation of comprehensive manuals covering airline operation.

To help achieve this within the timescale, stewardesses were press-ganged into duplicating and collating the necessary manuals, but it was deputy chief pilot Roy McDougall who, at the outset, accepted the brunt of the task.

As a line captain and latter-day manual salesman, he had no experience of paperwork or administration generally. The first need was for an operations manual.

Mike Forster, chief flight engineer, was given the task of pushing the manual along to secure the necessary Air Operator's Certificate. He still had his home in Bournemouth and, as a former BOAC Constellation flight engineer, he retained his manuals in the attic of the house there. He rushed down to the South Coast, brought the volumes back to Luton, deleted any references to BOAC, substituted Euravia, and handed the sheets out for typing.

Within the wooden shack which became Euravia's first Luton Airport base, there was one office for Williams, one for Harrington, and the rest shared a room – and one girl secretary. She could not possibly cope with all the input needed for that manual, so McDougall's wife, who was working elsewhere, typed much of it augmented by the other girls in her office who earned a few pounds by typing the sheets after hours.

Equally, several of the flight crew who were being taken on did not have Constellation experience, including McDougall who used the El Al book on the aircraft as his bible. What was learned from that, however, drew a blank from the examiners. It was not the appropriate background in the eyes of the British authorities who informed McDougall that they based their examinations on the Constellation input used by an airline called Trans-European Aviation who were flying these aircraft.

McDougall's visit to them drew a complete blank – they saw Euravia as a potential competitive threat and firmly declined any assistance. Fortunately, Trans-European's flight engineer, Andy McGill, was known within the Euravia camp. Like many flight crew in those days, his wife augmented his airline salary with a business of her own. In this case it was a hairdressing salon in Richmond, Surrey. Roy McDougall went to see McGill and he agreed to supply books and run classes for Euravia crew in the evening after the salon closed. It was certainly the strangest of aviation classrooms – men sitting under inactive hairdryers until 10.30pm on dark winter evenings learning the finer points of how to fly Constellations.

Euravia, in fact, had to satisfy several groups of people – the Air Transport Licensing Board, the officials who issued the Air Operator's Certificate, the Air Registration Board, and a plethora of other civil servants who had to be fed the relevant information in their pigeon-holes of activity.

As Jed Williams comments feelingly: "There was a whole bunch of

Chief flight engineer Mike Forster whose previous manuals proved invaluable for preparing the ground to obtain Euravia's first Air Operator's Certificate.

well-paid civil servants who had to be satisfied about something." Even so, he adds: "I must be fair to them. I think they all gave us a fair deal. At the time, I thought it very silly when we were all running around in small circles making sure the right piece of paper was signed by the right chap. Though they would heave everything in the book at us, I had the feeling that it would be all right on the night."

Another valuable hand to the AOC pump was given by Derek Davison after he had flown in the first of the Constellations from Israel.

"Though the certificate had not long been in force as a requirement in the UK, I soon realised that, nevertheless, it was not something to be dismissed as a light task," he reports. "It was quite a challenge, and all the time we had the aeroplanes and could not operate them we should be sitting on a pile of capital and not receiving any revenue."

The then Captain Davison's recollection of bringing that 'pile of capital', in the form of two 049 series Constellations and one series 149, is still vivid.

"We had a number of test flights on the Constellations in Israel before accepting delivery. To meet the required two-engine-out climb performance needed a delicate balance of bank angle to relieve the rudder and cowl grills, with oil cooler flaps closed to reduce drag to the point where both were on their temperature limits."

The actual flight for delivery of the first aircraft, Victor Papa, took 10¼ hours compared with the 4½ hours of today's modern jets. It was necessary to change the crystals in the radio set because of the then shortage of frequencies when passing through the Mediterranean towards Europe. The flight engineer on that delivery was Mike Forster, whose previous meeting with his captain had been seven years earlier when they both flew Comets for BOAC.

The last of those Constellation test flights in Israel was the day before departure for London Heathrow where formal clearance into the UK was to be given. Because the aircraft left Lod Airport, Tel Aviv, at 1.30am on April 11, 1962, it was a very tired Captain Davison who arrived back in England. Even then there was a mix-up over clearance, so Davison decided to call it a day rather than fly on to Luton as had originally been planned. As a result, his new boss Jed Williams was equally exhausted – he had been waiting at Luton for the historic arrival of his first aircraft.

This now took place the following morning, and it was the first time Captain Davison had landed at Luton.

"I remember feeling how green the countryside was after Israel – and also how difficult it was to spot the runway." By the time he brought the remaining two aircraft in, Echo November twelve days later, and X-ray Echo on May 12, he was beginning to feel at home.

Various shots of Constellations at Luton Airport. In all, Euravia took delivery of eight of the aircraft.

It was just a couple of weeks after delivery of the first aircraft that Captain Davison had a meeting with the Directorate of Aviation Safety to present them with the information for the all-important Air Operator's Certificate.

"We clearly had not done enough and we did not satisfy them. But before they said 'no', I jumped up and said: 'You want to see more of what we have done and be told less of what we are going to do.' The reply was that that was precisely right. I asked for another meeting in a week's time and we then got the certificate. If I had not done that, we might not have got the certificate at all."

When Chief Pilot Davison telephoned Deputy Chief Pilot McDougall to tell him of the award, McDougall was with fellow captain Frank Brown. Before joining Euravia, McDougall had been out of work for five months and during that period he had determined he was not going to drink until he got a job. The total abstinence was still in force when he received that phone call, but such was the relief and joy at the chief pilot's message that McDougall and Brown devoured half a bottle of whisky at one go. The two captains climbed to Cloud Nine very rapidly indeed.

But getting that certificate was just one railhead reached from a marshalling yard of activity still required to achieve first flight. Another was training the crews and converting many of them to a new type of aircraft as well as carrying out various checks. There were two aspects to checking the pilots. One was the normal line flying – familiarity with route, heights, navigational aspects and the whole scenario surrounding whether a pilot can fly safely. The other is the ability to deal with an engine failure, a three-engine landing, an engine fire, or, if necessary, evacuating the aircraft of its passengers. There was also parallel work to be done in engineering terms.

Derek Davison was working until one or two am, then facing an hour's drive home and snatching a few hours' sleep ready to be back in his Luton office by eight or nine the following morning. The reward for all this was the eventual awe-inspiring sight of that first flight taking off. Jed Williams and Derek Davison stood together near the old customs shed – still to be seen at Luton airport – on that fateful May day in 1962.

Davison still remembers it emotionally: "It was one of my proudest moments. We patted each other on the back and I said: 'We've made it. There she goes!'"

And so she did, but, as chief stewardess Marianne Allen remembers, the aircraft took off without oxygen masks on board. She asked the handling agent for some when they arrived at Manchester. He could produce only one – but fortunately the rest of the first flight was without incident.

Captain Don Tanton who operated Euravia's second flight when his Palma-bound passengers got no further than Barcelona.

Maybe that first flight was completed incident-free, but certainly not the second which took place on the same day. That took off in the early evening from Luton for Barcelona and Palma with 77 passengers under the command of Captain Don Tanton who, as the letter opposite shows, was recruited to Euravia on April 1 from Skyways. After half an hour's flying in rain, the windscreen-wipers stopped owing to a jammed motor. That was only a curtain-raiser, for at Barcelona the wheel brakes ceased to operate. It proved impossible to take the Palma passengers to their destination, so G-AHEN – 'hen' as the Constellation was affectionately known among the crew – limped back empty to Luton two days later.

As Jed Williams reflects: "On May 5, 1962 we still had not organised accounts, sales or supply departments. But we could fly and maintain our fleet. We could handle and cater for our passengers. We were earning revenue. In brief, the baby airline was born and very proud of it we all were!"

Another moment of pride occurred a few weeks later when Derek Davison went to St Athan in South Wales to see all three Constellations line up to take pilgrims to Lourdes. "The aircraft looked glorious, with the beautiful contours of their fuselages lined up one behind the other," he reflects.

To prove it was still early days for the airline, one of the captains on that charter did not even have a uniform!

In or out of uniform, everybody at Euravia was working extremely hard. For instance, the logbook for Captain Tanton shows that, seven weeks after the first flight, he left Luton five minutes after midnight in the third of the Constellation fleet, G-ARXE, with 67 passengers for Tenerife. The airfield at Tenerife North was notorious for early morning fog, and June 23 was no exception. Tanton circled around for two minutes short of two hours and then had to divert to Las Palmas because he was running out of fuel. The sun usually burned off the fog quite suddenly, and as he landed at Las Palmas, after 10¼ hours flying, Tanton was told by air traffic control that Tenerife was now clear. So he took off again, landed at Tenerife, and then departed with 65 passengers back to Luton where he touched down at 21.00 hours. Total duty time: 22 hours.

Though Don Tanton believes the Constellations did "a tremendous job", there was another occasion, in Valencia, when he could not start the number four engine. It was found that the fly-wheel would not engage with the crank-shaft. Tanton remembered that when he was flying Douglas Dakotas, the meshing could be achieved by pulling a chain underneath the engine. He suggested to his flight engineer David Brown – later to run the airline's training school – that, perhaps, there was a similar chain on the Constellation's engines. After taking all the cowlings off the engine, a lever was found on the back of the fly-wheel. The only way the engine could be started, however, was for Tanton to energise the starter from the cockpit while Brown actually stayed up in the engine and manually engaged the starter motor when it had reached the correct speed.

It was the hard work and willingness displayed in those early days that itself engendered a continuing spirit of enthusiasm, comradeship and humour. One early employee, Colette Smith, well remembered the atmosphere of that pioneering era.

"I recollect a strong feeling of friendship and fun from the very beginning. There was also a willingness on everyone's part to chip in and help each other – even if it was not in his or her job description. This was a major factor in contributing to the airline's success."

And Derek Davison pays warm tribute to the part Jed Williams played in fostering that spirit right from the start. "He introduced an effective culture of a positive kind which is still there today."

Down the line, this view was backed up by inventory control officer

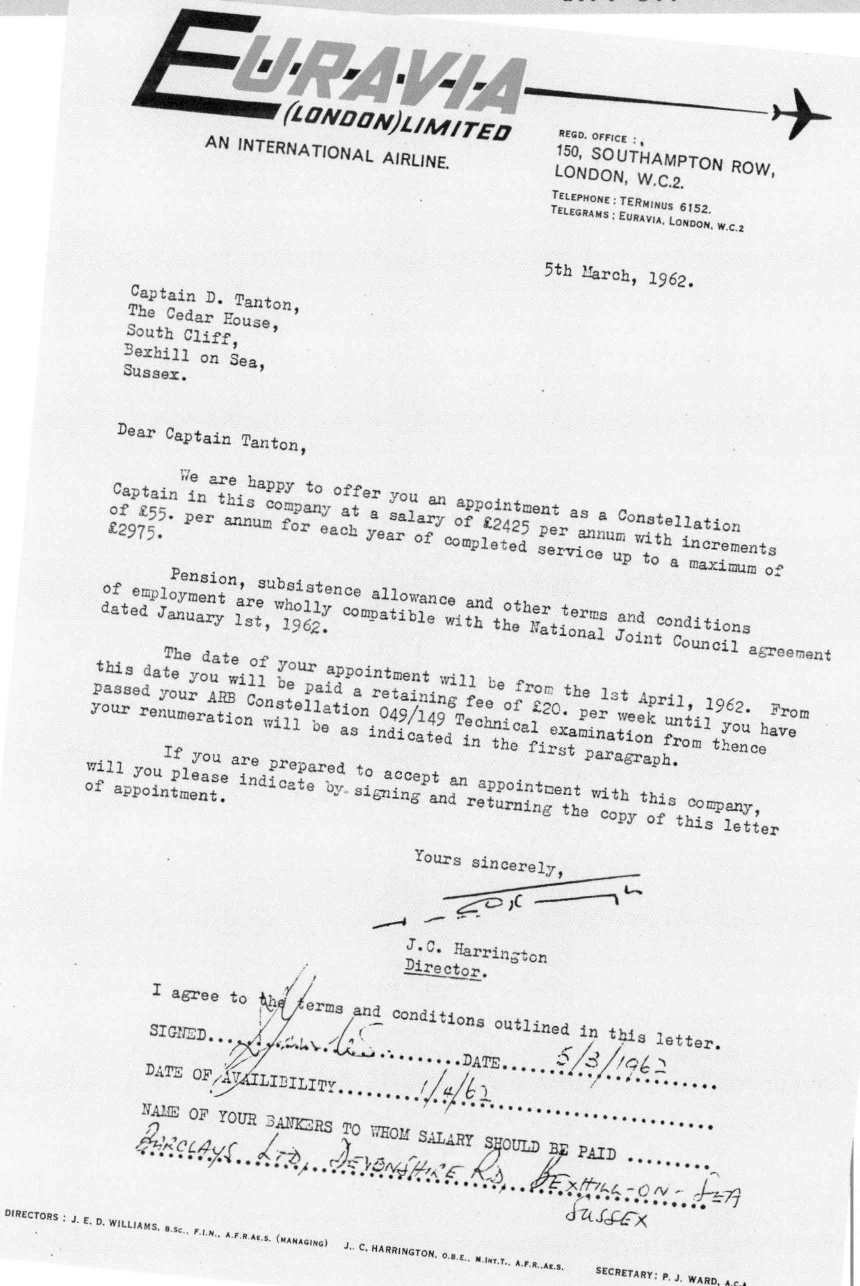
EURAVIA (LONDON) LIMITED
AN INTERNATIONAL AIRLINE.

REGD. OFFICE :
150, SOUTHAMPTON ROW,
LONDON, W.C.2.
TELEPHONE: TERMINUS 6152.
TELEGRAMS: EURAVIA, LONDON, W.C.2

5th March, 1962.

Captain D. Tanton,
The Cedar House,
South Cliff,
Bexhill on Sea,
Sussex.

Dear Captain Tanton,

We are happy to offer you an appointment as a Constellation Captain in this company at a salary of £2425 per annum with increments of £55. per annum for each year of completed service up to a maximum of £2975.

Pension, subsistence allowance and other terms and conditions of employment are wholly compatible with the National Joint Council agreement dated January 1st, 1962.

The date of your appointment will be from the 1st April, 1962. From this date you will be paid a retaining fee of £20. per week until you have passed your ARB Constellation 049/149 Technical examination from thence your renumeration will be as indicated in the first paragraph.

If you are prepared to accept an appointment with this company, will you please indicate by signing and returning the copy of this letter of appointment.

Yours sincerely,

J.C. Harrington
Director.

I agree to the terms and conditions outlined in this letter.
SIGNED........................DATE.......5/3/1962.......
DATE OF AVAILIBILITY.........1/4/62.........................
NAME OF YOUR BANKERS TO WHOM SALARY SHOULD BE PAID ....
BARCLAYS LTD, DEVONSHIRE RD, BEXHILL-ON-SEA SUSSEX

DIRECTORS : J. E. D. WILLIAMS, B.Sc., F.I.N., A.F.R.Ae.S. (MANAGING) J. C. HARRINGTON, O.B.E., M.Inst.T., A.F.R.Ae.S. SECRETARY: P. J. WARD, A.C.A.

◄ *Captain Tanton's letter of appointment to Euravia showing the terms and conditions of the day.*

Charlie McEwan: "My strongest memories are of the energy and drive of all the workforce to make the new airline succeed. And I believe it was the high calibre of the first supervisory staff and their expertise which helped to make it the successful airline it is today."

And the early customers noticed. Bruce Tanner, who became chairman of Horizon Midlands, remembers the Constellation days.

"Like many 'prop' aircraft, they had frequent snags, but however one might describe those aircraft – and a wide variety of descriptions was used at the time – the operational staff always did their damndest to get things right, a tradition started by Jed Williams."

Tanner recalls once having to call up Williams in the middle of the night because a propeller had fallen off one of the Constellations in Venice.

But that was typical of the dedication of the Euravia team. Derek Davison and Roy McDougall established the spirit for the rest of the flight crew. They never minded getting out of bed in the night and undertaking a flight. There was no way any crew member could moan about having deskbound bosses.

"Derek really set an example and the crews were quick to pick it up," recalls McDougall. The chief pilot stamped out traditional malpractices of aircrew – he forbade the custom of the flight deck team being given brandies by a hostess on arrival back at their home airport, known as the 'After-landing drink'. Equally, if the cabin staff took so much as an apple from the supplies on leaving the aircraft – and scavenging remaining stocks is still a big problem for many airlines – Derek Davison told them they would be fined immediately. He also stopped the other old Spanish custom of crews being allowed to retain half their hotel allowance if they returned to the UK rather than staying overnight at distant outstations.

'I think, in the end, this kind of discipline went a long way to building up the spirit of the airline," says Roy McDougall.

Within that spirit, there developed plenty of characters. One, whom no one among the early flying crew will ever forget, earned the nickname 'Fag-end Lil'. Euravia had recruited several 'mature' hostesses because of the difficulties of enticing staff to Luton. 'Lil', like everyone else, would work all hours, but she loved her cigarette. As soon as she was within the confines of the galley, a cigarette was popped into a holder which was quickly inserted between her lips. When the flight deck asked for two cups of tea, she carried them both piping hot, in one leather-like hand – with that cigarette holder still projecting menacingly from her lips.

But, perhaps, the most mercurial characters of all were those Constellation aircraft which founded the first Euravia fleet.

Jed Williams' point about employing people who had learned to distrust those early Constellations is amply borne out by Derek Davison's memories of them.

"The Constellation was known to us in those days as the 'hydraulic monster' in recognition of the amount of hydraulic pipe-runs in the aircraft – all prone to leaks. Passengers slipped on hydraulic fluid as they ran to the aircraft – no seat allocation in those days! Whenever we visited RAF Lyneham hordes of airmen rushed out with drip trays and placed them in position around the aircraft."

Euravia's first hangar was a building shared with Vauxhall Motors. Here a wing of a Constellation is stretching over car components. The frequent result of this was that oil from the wings dripped on to the untreated metal giving it a rustproofing bonus.

Manchester Airport even allocated a dedicated stand for the oil-leaking Constellations because of the braking problems they created for other operators. At least those hydraulic leaks did somebody some good. In their earliest Luton Airport days, Euravia shared a building with Vauxhall Motors for use as a hangar. A chain-link fence down the middle separated car bodies and components from aircraft. To get a Constellation into the building, however, it was necessary for a wing to stretch for eight to ten feet beyond the fence, so it projected above piles of car bodies. The Vauxhall men had to come at intervals with wire brushes to remove the rust which had collected on the untreated metal of the car bodies. It was significant, however, that those components piled directly underneath the Constellation's wing had no traces of rust – they had been protected by the leaking hydraulic fluid.

Not because of the Constellations' peculiarities, but there was acute difficulty in enticing experienced engineers to come and work at Luton. This was allied to the fact that competent aviation engineers were thin on the ground, so, for checks after every 120 hours of flying, the Constellations were flown on a 'no-sooner-are-you-up-than-you-are-down' sector from Luton to aeronautical engineers Marshalls of Cambridge.

Equally, all the teeth-gnashings with the Constellations could not be entirely blamed on that idiosyncratic aircraft. Derek Davison was somewhat alarmed on one flight from South Africa when he glanced towards the righthand seat and noticed the first officer's shoes being eaten by an escaped lion cub!

CHAPTER FOUR

Gaining height

So the name Euravia in blue and black lettering on a white fuselage, in what today would be regarded as a somewhat inelegant typescript, could now be seen spread along the fuselage of Constellations G-ARVP, G-AHEN and G-ARXE at a growing number of European airports. But that did not mean that the company was also beginning to take-off in a corporate sense. A capital base of £25,000 offered precious little corporate liquidity or manoeuvrability with a growing staff, fuel costs, landing fees, and passenger, hangar, engineering and other facilities to be paid for.

The stark economic reality was that they were achieving around 1,200 hours a year of flying out of each of the Constellations. This was mainly within a short operational window because of the holiday market being, of necessity, concentrated on the summer months. A few weeks' flying to South America or the Middle East was about all that was available outside that, but for the rest of the winter the aircraft were in revenue-earning hibernation.

Though it was a case of scratching around for business to gain some aircraft hours during the winter, those months were not allowed to be completely wasted. Dennis Hull, assistant to the financial controller, remembered that it was a time for catching up on book-keeping. One period when there was certainly no flying was Christmas Day – and then the terminal building was turned to festivities with a staff party victualled by the airline's catering department.

Even so, things were so tight that when it became necessary to buy another engine for a Constellation, the money was simply not there. Jed Williams had to come to the rescue with a personal guarantee of £5,000.

Despite this, an opportunity for growth presented itself which could not be missed. The biggest charter company in Britain at that time was Skyways, long established, and operating three 749 series Constellations – much superior to Euravia's – and Avro York freighter aircraft. The airline was in trouble. Because these Constellations had a large door, Skyways had gained a long-range BOAC freighter charter contract to Hong Kong and Australia, but the State airline had now abruptly ended that work.

So only three months after their first flight, Euravia were in active discussion to take over Skyways, and were talking to Martins Bank which had a debenture for more than the company's assets could possibly realise.

Universal Sky Tours' chairman was Air Commodore Sidney Smith who was given the job by Ted Langton. It was Smith's duty to act as a 'front man' for the company. If there were any irate customers or inquisitive journalists, it was his task to deal with them because Langton hated the public relations aspect of business.

Sidney Smith had previously been employed by Skyways, and it was through that channel that the approach was made to Euravia. In addition to the charter airline, there was Skyways Engineering at Stansted Airport, which had diminished from whole aircraft overhaul to less ambitious component overhaul, and Skyways Coach Air which ran a ferry service across the English Channel. Despite the obvious decline, the company was still being run with style and corporate grandeur.

But now the day of reckoning had arrived. The creator of the deal which took the ailing company into Euravia was Victor Doel, Skyways' finance director. Firstly, Skyways Engineering was hived off for the benefit of Martins Bank. Though the coach-air operation did not have much future, Skyways owned the airfield they used at Lympne in Kent and that had real estate value.

One of the Constellation 749s, registration number G-ANUR, which Euravia inherited when it bought Skyway's Ltd.

There were traffic rights to Malta, though these were later sold to British European Airways. Even the lumbering Yorks brought contracts including an emergency service for Pan American to get spare engines to unserviceable aircraft stranded anywhere between Iceland and Iran.

The core company, Skyways Ltd., was sold to Euravia, with a £¼ million overdraft, for just £1. The deal was that Euravia employed the assets, and, after deducting their costs and making a contribution to overheads, the rest of the revenue went to reducing the overdraft.

Doel's deal turned out to be a good one for virtually all the parties concerned.

As Jed Williams comments: "About thirty British airlines had gone bankrupt since the war, and this was the only deal I am aware of where a civilised arrangement was made resulting in everyone being better off. The shareholders and the unsecured creditors all received something out of it, and Martins Bank – later taken over by Barclays – got most of their money back."

There was a postscript to the deal, as Williams recalls:

"We had a lot of static from the Air Transport Licensing Board because of our lack of capital against the ambitions of our plans, having doubled the size of the fleet in the first four months. Any change in the share capital would, of course, have diluted my 20 per cent holding in Euravia. So the aircraft which originally belonged to Universal Sky Tours had their titles transferred to the airline during the first year, and Euravia paid the £90,000 by an instrument of subordinated debt that kept the ATLB happy because now £115,000 was shareholders funds instead of £25,000."

Incidentally, there was a good personal tailpiece for Jed Williams himself. He bought the business of Skyways Engineering from Martins Bank, with money which Martins loaned him, turned it into the Canford group of companies, and sold it to advantage to Rio Tinto Zinc in 1983.

But, most important of all, these events created a new dimension to Euravia. That is a view to which Derek Davison strongly subscribes: "Skyways was a real turning point in the company's history. It more than doubled the size of the airline in one sweep, and it told the public that this small company was here to stay. I think it was very much a stepping-stone to the next stage."

But before that, there was the question of assimilating Skyways' staff into their new parentage. Though there was, for instance, no equivalent opening for either the Skyways' operations director or its chief pilot, both readily accepted positions as line captains. Not only that, they gave strong

▲ *Euravia also took over the Avro York fleet of Skyways. This aircraft, G-AGNV, was sold to the Staverton museum.*

support to their new superiors.

Hardly was the ink dry on the Skyways coup than another operator of a couple of Constellations, Trans-European Aviation, also became financially embattled, and that well-known City of London corporate disaster doctor, Sir Kenneth Cork, was appointed receiver. The arrangement that Williams came to with him was to lease Trans-European's two Constellations for £20 an hour, with a guaranteed minimum of 600 hours' flying a year.

Euravia, therefore, rapidly grew from a three-Constellation operation to a company with eight Constellations and two Yorks. Though Jed Williams adds the reminder with feeling:

"The Constellations had high direct operating costs, poor mechanical reliability, and were slower than the Douglas DC6s and DC7s of the competition. They were not attractive to charterers – the reason we acquired them on such advantageous terms. The Yorks would already have been scrap were it not for that valuable Pan Am contract.

"There was no possibility of making much profit, but without any investment we were developing a viable business, not dependent on Universal Sky Tours, in preparation for the next stage which would be profitable." In fact, at no time did Williams allow Sky Tours to account for more than half of his total bookings.

But the next stage would need money. And that, Williams discovered, presented a problem. At the launch of Euravia, Universal Sky Tours' bank had required that the airline use only them as bankers. Initially, that did not seem unreasonable, but a limit had been placed on the overdraft facilities for the group. And with Ted Langton acquisitive to buy his own hotels, as well as the needs of organic growth, Universal Sky Tours grabbed every penny of overdraft for itself.

Jed Williams confesses: "The problem was how to build up an airline without using money, and at the same time provide Sky Tours with low-priced transport of acceptable standard to enable Langton to realise his plans. Those plans were, of course, important to us, too, but also they were the only reason he formed the airline in the first place – and the source of the only interest he ever showed in it.

"Naturally, I consulted him about every major step, but all he ever said was, at worst, 'I hope you know what you are doing,' or, at best, 'You seem to know what you are doing.' Ted Langton was precisely the patron the airline needed in those days. He starved us of cash and was our most demanding customer. Within the restraint of these excellent disciplines, I could develop the airline as I pleased so long as nothing went seriously wrong."

There were certainly one or two very narrow escapes from serious operational incident. Roy McDougall was taking a Constellation from Luton to Munich, and then onwards to Rome, with a planeload of Americans. For some unexplainable reason, McDougall felt uneasy on the Munich–Rome sector and insisted on going through half an hour's emergency drill with his first officer. When approaching Rome, as was normal practice, the auto-pilot was disengaged for a manual landing. The captain suddenly spotted that his co-pilot was constantly winding the trim forward in order to keep the aircraft level. Suddenly, there was a twanging sound and the aircraft began to dive. In this situation, the action is to let go of the controls – not an instinctive thing to do. Then, to take pressure off, the 'walking stick' boost control level has to be pulled up. McDougall yelled at his first officer to let go of the controls, but as his mind concentrated on the crisis in hand, the last McDougall now remembers is that the plane went into a vertical dive.

Realising it was not a flying control problem, the auto-pilot having failed to disengage, what he next recalled was the aircraft climbing steeply and needing trimming the other way. McDougall then flew the aircraft using the trimmer and not the controls. Once the Constellation was under control, having given three 'mayday' distress broadcasts, McDougall called Rome air traffic control to ask whether they had a tape of the incident.

They had obviously not received the 'mayday' calls and could not understand what was now being requested. After asking the captain for a repeat of the inquiry, the controller answered innocently in broken English: "Yes, we do have a tap here if you want a drink when you land."

On another occasion Derek Davison was captaining a Constellation taking freight down to Nairobi in Kenya. On the way back, he was detailed to pick up a couple of engines which had been overhauled in Israel. It was an established fact that if a pilot were to fly over an Arab country, he did not indicate that his destination was Tel Aviv. Consequently, Davison asked for clearance to Nicosia, Cyprus.

However, unknown to him, the airline's agent in Nairobi, having seen a signal from Luton about picking up the engines, in all innocence mentioned this in the clearance procedure.

Deputy chief pilot Roy McDougall who recalls many interesting and unusual flights in the early days.

The result was that as soon as the Constellation crossed into Egyptian airspace, Captain Davison was peremptorily told to leave. He did not need asking twice and, instead, flew along the Egyptian border into Libyan territory. In those days, Libyan air traffic control was fairly relaxed, and so the Constellation made its way to Cypriot control. Davison decided it would be a good idea to land in Nicosia and, rather than cause attention by employing an agent, he used the step ladder to leave the aircraft, paid £20 directly in fees, and took off as rapidly as possible for Tel Aviv to collect the engines. On other occasions when a step-ladder was not available, he remembers using the emergency escape rope from the front cockpit door. In fact, he laid claim to be the only Euravia captain who could shin up the rope back into the flight-deck.

There were, of course, many less hazardous and more relaxed missions in those Constellations. For instance, two of the aircraft were used in the weeks before Christmas, 1962, for a six-weeks tour by Martha Graham and her American ballet group accompanied by a 70-strong London orchestra. The performers, stage sets and musical instruments were flown to Ankara, Tel Aviv, Athens, Belgrade, Zagreb, Warsaw, Munich, Cologne, Stockholm, Oslo, Helsinki and Amsterdam.

Revenue-earning loads, however, did not always consist of passengers. The 749-type Constellations, taken over from Skyways, had freight doors, and among the consignments these carried was a ship's propeller rushed urgently from Copenhagen to Aden. And Aden was the airport to which another Constellation was diverted on its way back to England from the Far East to uplift several tons of silver coins, belonging to the 18th century Queen Maria Theresa of Hungary, for offloading in Milan.

The saddest sight for many at Luton was when the old Constellations were slowly towed up a slope around the perimeter of the airport to be broken up. In those days, technical director Bernard Newton was a line engineer, and he remembers one occasion when they wanted to retract an undercarriage on arrival at the 'graveyard'. Stubborn yet dignified to the last, the aircraft steadfastly refused to fall on its underbelly despite all the tugging and pushing of levers in the cockpit.

Not all the Constellations were broken up. The honour of being the last captain in the company to fly a Constellation went to now retired Jim Watret. The aircraft in question had a curiously tasteless interior trim – chromium fittings with gaudy gold, yellow and red coverings. As the last Constellation in the Luton fleet, it had been bought by an American, and Captain Watret was to take it to the customer via Shannon in Ireland. Struggling against a strong headwind, he reached the cruising height of 14,000 feet when the hydraulic fluid started going down rapidly. The flight engineer had to keep topping it up.

▲

Captain Jim Watret, the last Euravia pilot to fly a Constellation. The aircraft ended its life as a snack bar at Shannon Airport in Ireland.

◄▲

An ignominious and sad end for other Constellations in the Euravia fleet. These two aircraft, like others, were broken up on the perimeter of Luton Airport.

"Eventually we reached Shannon in the biggest pool of hydraulic fluid you have ever seen in your life," Jim Watret remembers.

That, however, was not the end of the story. The deal with the American fell through, and so the last of Euravia's Constellations became a snack bar just outside the gates of Shannon Airport.

Watret is the man who made one of the more printable jokes about the oil problems of the Constellations. Because the engines burned two or three gallons of oil an hour, it tended to cause a lot of smoke emission. One day, after leaving Luton, the air traffic controller called Watret on the radio to report there was a considerable amount of smoke coming from his number four engine.

"I can't understand that," retorted the captain. "I've got the no smoking signs on!"

BRITANNIA AIRWAYS
BRITANNIA AIRWAYS

Flying 'BY'

CHAPTER FIVE

If, as Derek Davison maintains, the acquisition of Skyways and its Constellations was a major step forward in the airline's evolution, then the next milestone event was a giant's stride – in fact, a 'Whispering Giant'. For that was the name given to the Britannia airliner, the most significant turbo-propeller aircraft ever built as far as performance and safety were concerned. In service with BOAC and El Al, it became the first aircraft capable of regularly flying the Atlantic non-stop and it was the quietness of its four Bristol Proteus engines that earned it the deserved sobriquet.

However, those engines were not all sweetness and quiet. To gain a compact power unit, the airflow through them was designed to be doubled back on itself. In the resulting 'u' curve, icing problems developed in the jet stream. The penalty, as a result of eradicating this, was late delivery which meant that when the Britannia entered service in 1957 on BOAC's African routes it had the shine of its competitive edge dimmed by the imminent arrival on the scene of the pure jet Boeing 707 and Douglas DC-8. BOAC later took delivery of the 310 series Britannias, with a ten foot longer fuselage, and having bought 18 of them at around £1 million each, they then mothballed all 14 of their earlier 102 series.

In the couple of years since the launch of Euravia, business had been increasing encouragingly. In that inaugural year of 1962, Euravia carried less than 20,000 passengers, but in 1963 this had grown to more than 50,000 using not only Luton, but Manchester, Newcastle and, to a lesser extent, Cardiff and Blackpool. And new routes were pioneered including one of today's most popular destinations, Ibiza.

With this broadened base, the Constellations were becoming less attractive, so much so that Jed Williams opened negotiations to buy some of those idle Britannias. The resulting deal meant that, for less than the cost of a new Britannia 310, he bought six of the earlier models together with engine spares on a 'buy now, pay later' scheme. Another two followed later.

When Jed Williams told Ted Langton that the contract was signed, he only had one question: was the seating plan, unlike the Constellations, the same for all six Britannias?

On being told it was, he made a perceptive demand which foreshadowed later thinking in aircraft passenger flow: "Right, I'll need a copy of the seating plan to put on the booking form so that my clients can apply for their seats when they book their holidays. You'll have to print the same plan on the back of the tickets so they can see what seats they have actually got. You can use it as a kind of boarding card if you like."

But before those forerunners of today's boarding card were printed, another issue had been exercising Jed Williams' mind. He considered Euravia a "lousy name for an airline". Not only that, Britain was still many years off membership of the European Common Market and there were divisions in the country over the whole advisability of joining. So, perhaps, a pan-European sounding name was also not a propitious marketing title. What better to mark the new Britannia aircraft era than to adopt the name Britannia? So, on August 16, 1964, Euravia (London) Limited became Britannia Airways.

"It is the most extraordinary thing that the name was available," confesses Jed Williams. "Everyone wanted to have a name that did not sound like any other in the industry and suggested a responsible airline. We found that the name Britannia was lying there to be picked up."

Changing the name from Euravia to Britannia – the new flight desig-

◄

Opposite. *A new type of aircraft, the Bristol Britannia, entered the airline fleet. In the same year, 1964, Euravia changed its name to Britannia Airways.*

➤

The original Memorandum and Articles of Association following the formation of Britannia Airways.

THE COMPANIES ACT, 1929
and
THE COMPANIES ACT, 1948

COMPANY LIMITED BY SHARES

Memorandum

(Altered by Special Resolution passed 14th June, 1965)

AND

Substituted

Articles of Association

(Adopted by Special Resolution passed 14th June, 1965)

OF

Britannia Airways Limited.

ALLEN & OVERY,
9-12 Cheapside,
London, E.C.2.

nation was BY – created one baffling incident. A huge bundle of invoices for fuel was received at Luton from Cairo. This was not a Britannia destination airport, but, as the bills were in Arabic, it was difficult to pinpoint them. The only clue was the aircraft registrations – and on checking they all turned out to belong to BOAC. The fuel suppliers at Cairo had read about Britannia Airways and thought it was the new name for Britain's State airline.

The 112-seat Britannia aircraft, under the banner of Britannia Airways, became a real success story. As the new Britannia fleet touched down at Luton, the valiant Constellations were, in the case of the original three, scrapped, and others handed back to the receivers of Skyways and Trans-European Aviation.

As chief pilot, Derek Davison was in charge of crew conversion. "It was a very considerable change, not too much in handling since the Britannia, like the Constellation, had propellers. It was halfway between a piston and a jet aircraft, but we had to learn the most economical cruise procedures, and there were risks of engine failure when flying at lower altitudes and compressor damage when ice broke off. But we achieved a pretty good record."

That record was undoubtedly aided by the fact that both Jed Williams and Derek Davison had been operating Britannias with El Al. And they had been doing so very successfully – more so than BOAC. They had mastered the aircraft and how to fly it, achieving better timetables on the North Atlantic. This earned them one newspaper headline: "Britannia

Rules the Air – thanks to El Al".

Britannia flight crew technical training was undertaken for Britannia by BOAC in their Cranebank school at Heathrow Airport. The first candidates for flying training on the 102 type were Captain Davison and Captain Tanton who were instructed by Bristol Aeroplane's test pilot Willie Williamson. The two captains undertook the airline's inaugural Britannia flight from Luton on December 6, 1964, carrying pre-Christmas holiday-makers seeking Tenerife's winter sun. But, returning the next day, they had to redirect to Heathrow owing to strong crosswinds at their Luton base.

The Britannia gave the airline another opportunity for a 'first'. They became the first charter company to provide in-flight hot meals. The staple diet in those days was cottage pie, and its aroma often greeted passengers as they entered the cabin. "I can smell the pie" became a regular remark of passengers.

Perhaps with an eye to taking the cuisine up-market, the caterers decided to change the dish's name to 'Italian Cottage Pie'. When incensed passengers wrote to the press indignantly asking why Italian food was being served, the ethnic description was quickly deleted.

Some of the most vivid memories of the airline's flight crews flying Britannias was of the charter work they carried out for Iran Air, taking Moslems to Mecca for the annual pilgrimage of the Hadj.

In his flying career, spanning 41 years, Roy McDougall flew no less than 21,854 hours, but few of them were more intensive than those Hadj assignments. In just one month, April 1966, he had 16 flights totalling 114 hours. These were mainly return trips home for the pilgrims to various destinations in Iran such as Tehran, Shiraz and Abadan. Not only did McDougall have to keep a beady eye out for attempts to overload the aircraft at Jeddah, but the exodus was complicated by an outbreak of typhoid so that those infected had to take pills and wait two days before they could return.

In addition to the passengers, the returning aircraft carried holy water from Mecca, but Alan Johnson, one of the other captains on that run, remembers a more secular water problem. One Britannia appeared extraordinarily heavy and developed a great reluctance to take-off from Jeddah. It was discovered that the bottom of the aeroplane had been filled with water. Mistake or otherwise, the aircraft had to be emptied. The drain holes, which normally close with air pressure, were kept open with the aid of match-sticks, and the water emptied out during flight.

One of the biggest operations undertaken by Britannia in the mid-sixties (below left) *was flying Muslim pilgrims to Mecca for the annual Hadj. Captain Alan Johnson* (below) *discovered that his Britannia aircraft had mysteriously developed considerable extra weight on one of these holy flights.*

Many of the Mecca pilgrims came from Morocco. Here one party is seen returning to Rabat.

For the crew, the Hadj run involved a ten hours on – ten hours off working day. "A good way to kill yourself," Roy McDougall reflects ruefully.

He does remember one day in Shiraz when there were two hours to spare.

A beautiful Persian girl, who was the local-speaking member of the flight crew, suggested she take the rest of the team to see the sights, including the famous blue mosque. Six of them piled into a taxi, only to be stopped by a policeman. An argument ensued between the law and the girl who informed the rest dejectedly: "It's no good. He's fined us for overloading the taxi." They had a whip-round and paid the fine on-the-spot whereupon the girl told them to get back into the taxi. "We can't do that," protested McDougall. "He'll do us again."

"Oh no," replied the girl disarmingly. "A fine is good for twelve hours," whereupon they enthusiastically re-started their tour of the mountain-rimmed town.

The Middle East was also the backcloth for another Britannia anecdote. One of the contracts won for Britannia aircraft was to fly troops to Singapore over Christmas. Bahrain was a staging stop, and in those days there were not the modern luxury hotels available today. Roy McDougall found himself staying in a windowless room of an hotel in an Arab quarter of the city. He became suspicious of his air conditioning, traced it back, and found the source of the supply was a dormitory sleeping twenty people from which the air was frozen and pumped directly into his room.

Captain André Jeziorski, a Pole who also joined the airline from Skyways after escaping from France during World War Two to join RAF Coastal Command, holds the distinction of being the only pilot in the company to fly a Britannia on just two engines, both on the same wing.

He had taken inclusive tour passengers to Venice from England during which trouble had developed with the propellers on one of the outer engines. It was found to be a serious technical problem on arrival in Italy. Luton refused to give permission to return on three engines, instead detailing engineers to fly out and fix the problem. They found on arrival that they could not solve the malfunction without further equipment, so it was eventually agreed that Jeziorski would fly the aircraft back empty to Luton on three engines.

Unfortunately, just before reaching Paris on the return, the adjoining

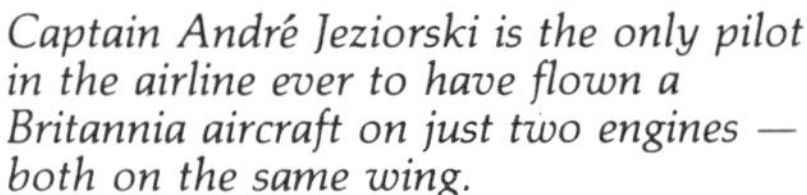

Captain André Jeziorski is the only pilot in the airline ever to have flown a Britannia aircraft on just two engines — both on the same wing.

inboard engine also developed problems. To aggravate the situation, there was a cross-wind and rain at Luton, but the Pole's skill ensured a safe touchdown.

Another three-engined ferry flight, from Athens, is remembered by its captain, Derek Davison. After flying for a couple of hours, a shadow suddenly came across the cockpit and, instinctively, he and the flight engineer, Mike Forster, ducked. Shadows at cruising height do not cross cockpits, and the thought was of another aircraft about to crash into them. The real reason for the shadow had a simple explanation – the lowering sun had shone on to the feathered propeller of the inactive engine and it had at that precise moment made one involuntary rotation. "It was quite amazing how worried we got," Davison admits.

One VIP tour Captain Jim Watret clearly remembers is taking Edward Heath on a Far Eastern tour when the ex-Prime Minister was Leader of the Opposition. It was just after Christmas and, following visits to India and Brunei, the Britannia developed an engine failure. When Watret signalled Luton, he was instructed to charter another aircraft at virtually whatever the cost. Meanwhile, however, Heath had persuaded Malaysian Airlines to take him on to Saigon.

Captain Watret then flew the Britannia back to Calcutta where it was exchanged for another aircraft which had been sent out from Luton. He made for Saigon arriving in time to hear that Indian Prime Minister Shastri had died, so the plane had to return to Delhi with Mr Heath for the funeral. The whole trip took two weeks, and it was demanding in another way – invariably Edward Heath wanted two soft boiled eggs for breakfast!

Britannia Airways needed to gain more utilisation out of its fleet. With the gradually lengthening duration, and greater liberalisation of timing, for workers taking holidays in Britain, Jed Williams suggested to Ted Langton that he could offer him lower rates for flights which left UK airports or returned to them in mid-week rather than at the peak-demand weekends. As a result, Langton came up with an 11 to 12-day holiday for which passengers left midweek and returned at the weekend, or vice versa.

This development was, theoretically, superb for both travel company and airline but, in practice, it came up against the British Government bureaucrats' own Berlin Wall. Firstly, there was what was termed Provision 1. This proclaimed that no packaged holiday could be offered at a lower price than the normal economy scheduled return air fare to that particular destination's airport. Secondly, the Air Transport Licensing Board had traditionally supported the scheduled carriers' view that charter traffic diverted passengers from their services.

Jed Williams had, for long, strongly put forward his belief that this stand was untenable.

"The point I kept making was that our product was not like a scheduled airline ticket to, say, Palma. Our product was sea, sun, sand and secondary sexual stimulation. And that was a completely different product from anything the State airlines had ever dreamt of offering. We were not in the same line of business and, therefore, not competing. This was my argument before them for a very long time."

The need was to secure what was called a 'B' licence. Again, for the new concept, Williams was his own chief advocate as he had been for the original licences three years earlier. There was a plethora of protests led vigorously by Henry Marking, the chief executive, on behalf of British European Airways.

When Williams was not fighting for his own corner, the spirited attack was kept up by Donald McQueen, an ex-Royal Navy commander, who had been sales manager for the original Skyways company and retained the same role for Britannia gaining many ad hoc charters. When the Air Transport Licensing Board finally conceded the merits of the

▲

The graceful lines of the Bristol Britannias, as seen in the top picture, acquire a less appealing aspect on being broken up for scrap at Luton. During their service with the airline, they had been very popular aircraft with both passengers and crews.

airline's case in 1965, BEA appealed not just against Britannia's licences but against those granted to all the independents.

Jed Williams decided this was the time to assume leadership of the independents in their battle, and so, for the first time, he employed professional advocacy in Geoffrey Rippon, QC, who had been a Minister of Aviation in the Conservative Government.

"Rippon was a delight to work with," says Williams. "Having disposed both of the State corporation's case and its counsel, he demanded costs on the High Court scale against the corporation, unheard of then, for wasting everyone's time. That was turned down, but the central argument for restricting 'B' licences, otherwise than under Provision 1, was abandoned for ever. The practical significance was that we had security of tenure and security of the right to grow."

So incensed was Jed Williams about the whole background to the need for this kind of application that he once wrote for Flight magazine:

"The first delusion is that aviation is in some special way connected with national prestige and the national interest.

"The second delusion is that air transport is a delicate plant which needs careful regulation and control if it is to grow up sturdily. Nothing could be further from the truth. In the first place it is big business; the world's airlines turn over thousands of millions annually. In the second place the regulatory bodies do not nurture it; they throttle it. No case can be made that control is in the interest of the nation, the travelling public, or the industry. The world is full of sane business men anxious and willing to provide the risk capital to operate public services, given the freedom to do so.

"It is strange that people who are not doctrinaire socialists of the old school and whose general philosophy and political orientation is towards a limited laissez faire in a capitalist society believe that British civil aviation, for some reason, needs to be strangled by red tape in a manner unparalleled in any other industry of modern Western society. Aviation is no different from any other industry of comparable magnitude and importance. It follows the common economic rules and reacts in the same way to commercial stimuli and government control."

No doubt that 'unparalleled red tape' phrase was underlined by Jed Williams' experience in the very summer of the airline's start-up when they were working flat-out to keep the business afloat. One day, he discovered that, at the same time, his sales manager was giving evidence at an ATLB hearing; the company secretary was engaged with Ministry of Aviation accountants charged with reporting to the ATLB on their financial affairs; the operations superintendent was with a flight operations inspector of the Directorate of Aviation Safety; the chief pilot was engaged with a training inspector of the Directorate of Aviation Safety; the chief engineer was with ARB surveyors concerned with the maintenance schedules of the Constellations; and the chief inspector was busy with another ARB surveyor concerned with Air Operator's Certificates.

The year 1965, thanks to the lifting of those restrictions through the Air Transport Licensing Board victory, was another turning point for Britannia Airways and was also crucially significant for the airline in a more direct corporate context.

Changing course

CHAPTER SIX

Hamlet in his 'To be, or not to be' soliloquy speaks of "a consummation devoutly to be wished". In 1965, the heads of two disparate organisations were echoing those sentiments.

There was no doubt that by then Jed Williams was increasingly feeling that Britannia Airways had reached a stage where the existing structure had to come to an end. To use his phrase: "Life with Ted Langton was rather hairy."

Though Williams readily concedes that Langton was a brilliant thinker about travel, and knew the business inside out, "he had no management skills whatsoever and no understanding of the need for those skills." As an example, the man who kept the general ledger was not a qualified accountant and there was no one managing the group cash flow. Universal Sky Tours would suddenly stop paying its bills because Langton had impulsively gone out and bought another hotel.

"Ted was a one-man mafia operating from a completely separate building, and there was no real control. From my point of view, this was terribly worrying and very frightening," says Williams.

To aggravate the situation, Langton was into his sixties and had already had heart trouble. The stark reality was that if he died, Britannia could well have been put into the hands of a receiver in a matter of weeks.

"Though Ted had told me that if anything happened to him there was only me to handle his group, there was no way I could deal with it because nobody knew the crucial facts of the business as nothing was on file or recorded. If a hotel, for instance, said Sky Tours owed them some money, nobody but Ted knew what the exact liabilities were. The airline could go bankrupt because Ted could have left a nought off one of the sums he worked out on the back of an envelope."

Gordon Brunton was in 1965 asked by Lord Thomson to find the most suitable diversification for his company. The final choice had to include six 'magical' ingredients.

So there was at that time a 'devout wish' on the part of Jed Williams for a sale of Universal Sky Tours and Britannia into an appropriate corporate setting which could encompass its managerial and growth needs.

If Williams' thinking could be looked upon as a north pole seeking a magnetic attraction, then the south pole was represented by the pressing needs of Gordon Charles Brunton. Each was oblivious to the ambitions of the other.

Brunton was a director of the International Thomson Organisation in Britain. His boss, Roy Thomson, had arrived in the UK from his native Canada late in life and purchased The Scotsman as the forerunner of a whole series of newspaper acquisitions which reached its prestigious climax with The Sunday Times, The Times, and a peerage.

Along the path of the printed word, however, he had strayed to good purpose into television. Having the Scottish Television franchise he had openly described as a "licence to print money". Unfortunately he eventually lost that lucrative licence. What he wanted urgently in 1965 was another business which would give him a positive cash flow.

By many standards, the group's financial resources were limited, so the search was for a business with short and long-term objectives: to create quickly a significant new profit centre at relatively low cost, and to lay the foundations for a big profit earner of the future where the development costs would not be high, at least in the beginning.

So Gordon Brunton was deputed to find an industrial elixir to incorporate six magical ingredients. He later listed them as: relatively low initial investment; an area not needing too much technical know-how – which virtually pre-supposed a service industry; substantial growth potential; an area where Thomson's skills, particularly in marketing, could contribute; an operation with a different cash-flow from that of newspapers, which was poor early in the year and at its best at the end of the year; and a business which could use the organisation's newspapers and magazines to deliver messages to consumers at a low cost.

Brunton could well have been reminded of the Book of Proverbs which asserts that 'whoso findeth a wife findeth a good thing'. His problem was to find a potential corporate 'wife' who had all those six attributes to make it suitable for marriage into the house of Thomson.

The young, nubile industry Gordon Brunton eventually courted was the package holiday business. He decided it was a good prospect on several grounds. A few entrepreneurs had seen the opportunities in packaged holidays, but had really only paddled by its shoreline because they did not have the financial resources to dive in more deeply. It was clear that holidays for workers in Britain were going to become longer and more frequent, aided by higher discretionary income for leisure spending. Jet aircraft had already entered the skies, and there was no doubt that they were the pathfinders for cheaper, faster and more efficient commercial air transport. It was pretty obvious to a man steeped in publishing that the increasing attention to travel abroad, both through the printed word and television, could strike a responsive chord, if the charges were low enough, in many more people resigned to sheltering under dripping umbrellas on some windswept English seafront.

The Thomson board accepted the Brunton recommendation; now the need was for quick action to find the right vehicle or vehicles to enter that fledgling inclusive tour business.

A pioneer in the business, along with Ted Langton, had been Vladimir Raitz who built Horizon Holidays. Brunton and he had been together at the London School of Economics. But Raitz, on being approached, expressed no interest in selling, instead suggesting a talk to Ted Langton.

Langton was happy to be wooed. His philosophy was that everything had a price. For Brunton it turned out easier to court Langton than was the case later with the Thomson board who had a distaste for buying 'hardware'. Those Britannia aircraft, which they were to acquire as assets, gave them the shudders.

They sent investigators up to Luton who were given a profit projection for the airline of £180,000 for 1965. But despite this, all sorts of objections were raised by members at the board meeting to discuss the potential purchase. It was even suggested that fixed-wing planes might eventually give way to helicopters to which someone responded facetiously: "Or camels." Some time afterwards, in his autobiography 'After I was Sixty', Lord Thomson, a man addicted to reading balance sheets as a hobby, confessed he didn't think he had ever heard a less favourable report than the one the accountants gave that day on the whole Langton business.

When Brunton retired from the Thomson Organisation (as Sir Gordon), he recalled the atmosphere surrounding the recommendation to go for Universal Sky Tours and another small operator, Riviera Holidays.

"Neither of the companies had ever made a profit, and in 1965 it was the very, very early days of the package tour business.

"Accountants Price Waterhouse moved in to investigate the books of both companies. The reports could scarcely have been worse. I shall never forget that meeting on the top floor of Elm House in Gray's Inn Road, London.

"I remember giving my views on why I thought there was a great opportunity for the future. Price Waterhouse responded with a formidable report analysing the companies' appalling performance, their totally unconventional, unstructured management style, their total lack of a track record, our complete inexperience of that business, and they put forward an unanswerable case. The marketing director jumped in, had his two-penn'orth, rejecting the whole crazy idea.

"It was then up to Roy Thomson to take the decision. He listened carefully and had, up to that point, not opened his mouth. He said very quietly and very simply, and I'll never forget those words: 'I think Gordon may be right. We shall go.' We did."

So the two businesses were bought, Universal Sky Tours costing, in total, £900,000. The signatures of agreement had to be applied rapidly because the then Wilson Government had announced the introduction of capital gains tax, and a deadline had to be met to avoid the sellers having to yield a hefty portion of their cash rewards to the Exchequer.

There is no doubt that, initially, the airline continued to be a niggling worry to those Thomson board members, as Sir Gordon explained more recently:

"When we went into the travel business, International Thomson was in the middle of a major reorganisation of its newspapers which was making enormous demands on our capital resources – we had re-machined the Sunday Times and were modernising all the run-down provincial newspapers. So there would be a great deal of concern about buying more hardware in the form of aeroplanes.

"Another difficulty was much more market-based. I, in particular, had always set my sights against vertical integration in our business. With newspapers you had to own printing works because of the speed of the process, but I had refused to own printing plants to print our books or magazines. So it seemed to my colleagues that the inclusion of Britannia was a dangerous form of vertical integration. But when I looked into it, I realised it was essential because you had to regard the travel side and the airline as one profit centre. I did manage to persuade my colleagues, though they were certainly reluctant."

So the person who, in Jed Williams' opinion, was the most fascinating man he had ever met, Ted Langton, did a deal with the man Gordon Brunton said was the most fascinating man he had met, Roy Thomson – Brunton diplomatically admitted to Williams that he regarded Langton as

Lord Thomson about to take his first flight as the new owner of Britannia Airways. The chief ground stewardess with him is Lavinia Wellicombe — later to become Mrs Derek Davison.

Lord Thomson, followed by Gordon Brunton, all smiles after leaving the Bristol Britannia aircraft. His takeover of the airline heralded a change in its fortunes in a very positive way.

the *second* most fascinating.

Jed Williams' view of the sale is that it was "wonderful" from virtually all points of view.

"Ted's deal with Thomson left everyone better off – the employees of Britannia Airways, the shareholders of the Thomson Organisation, the British public, the Iberian economy, and later the Boeing Airplane Company – to name but a few. Everyone, that is, except possibly Ted. The deal brought him a Berkshire estate, a string of thoroughbred horses, a flat in Grosvenor Square, and a large Mediterranean yacht, but they may have been a poor exchange for that backroom in Piccadilly from which Ted was exiled for ever by his success."

One annoyance for Ted Langton was that part of the deal was related to earnings in future years up to a certain maximum. Because of the continuing success of Britannia, that limit was reached within just two years.

Those colleagues of Gordon Brunton certainly saw their mentor breathtakingly vindicated when the final purchase price of the Langton deal was recouped within just one year. Apart from valuable cash flow generation, Thomson inherited, in the airline, what turned out to be a highly attractive return on investment in terms of projected price earnings ratios, eventually leading to profits of up to £30 million a year on a paid-up share capital of only £115,000. With that record, Jed Williams maintains it is the most successful venture ever in European air transport, an industry notoriously ineffectual in terms of return on investment.

For Gordon Brunton, the potential in the airline was visible from the very beginning.

"The first man I met in Britannia was Jed Williams who was very professional, very entrepreneurial, very efficient, and very ambitious. And my first impression of Britannia Airways was also one of efficiency – it was run like a battleship and still is. I have never changed that view. That was in great contrast to the travel company which was run by people with a great deal of creative flair who understood their markets, but with no managerial ability at all. It was an extraordinarily badly run business."

The significance of the Thomson-Langton deal, as far as the future of Britannia Airways was concerned, is summed up by Derek Davison, later to become its chairman and chief executive.

"The advent of Thomson was a change in the fortunes of the company in a very positive way. There was limitation at that time to the potential growth of the company because airlines were moving into an era requiring significant capital. To be able to expand was going to be extremely difficult in the company as it stood on its own. Against that, I suppose there was the loss of freedom which had come about with the setting up of a really, really independent airline. We were now part of a massive conglomerate organisation."

Going with Boeing

CHAPTER SEVEN

If the directors of the International Thomson Organisation had swallowed hard before being persuaded to purchase those aircraft assets of Britannia Airways, they could, perhaps, be forgiven for almost choking less than a year later over the request that Jed Williams brought to Gordon Brunton.

During the take-over negotiations, Williams and his team had assured Brunton and his colleagues that the Bristol Britannias they were flying were excellent aircraft to serve the needs of the airline for several years to come. There would be no need for ITOL, as the parent company is known to its directors and employees, to consider further capital expenditure on new aircraft in the foreseeable future.

What had happened to shatter that view was the rapid growth of the commercial jet age. It had dawned in July 1949, with the first flight of the de Havilland Comet, but had by the sixties, through such aircraft as the Douglas DC-9 and the BAC One-Eleven, reached the stage where pure jet aircraft were becoming highly competitive economically for inclusive tour work.

As Derek Davison explains: "For us, it was all about productivity. From the days of the Constellations with 82 passengers, taking eight hours to Palma and back, we moved to the Britannias with 112 passengers taking six hours, to what now became possible – carrying 117 passengers in just four hours. It made jolly good economic sense, particularly with the ability to achieve around 2,600 hours a year of flying out of the then modern jets."

So when Williams went along to Brunton's office with the news that Britannia wanted to buy a fleet of jet aircraft, he was somewhat forcefully reminded of that view so recently stated about the potential longevity of the turbo-prop Britannias.

Sir Gordon recalls: "When Jed admitted he had said that, he added: 'But can't you take a joke?', I retorted that it was not a very funny joke because the group at that time was very, very stretched. But I told him to sit down and talk me through it, whereupon Jed explained to me that there was a new generation of aircraft coming. They were not yet proven, but there was a clear indication that competition was going to grow and that the old concepts of comfort and flying were going to disappear. He convinced me they needed the new aeroplanes.

"The case seemed to me to be impressive, but I certainly got a frosty reception when I put it to the rest of the Thomson board who were very publishing dominated. I was responsible for travel and all the new diversified interests of Thomson, and they could see that if I was going to get aeroplanes they were not going to have their new printing presses, machines, cars, vans or whatever else they wanted."

The conflict in priorities was certainly not helped when it was revealed that the aircraft Britannia had in mind had not only never flown, but was still on the drawing boards.

In those days, it was rare for a charter operator to order brand new aircraft, let alone state-of-the-art aeroplanes which were not proven. The tradition among these companies was to buy second-hand planes from the main scheduled airlines at a time when these were moving towards the obsolescent period of their operational life. They were not necessarily old in lifespan terms, but they were beginning to be superseded, so that charter airlines could buy them at lower capital cost. By increasing the utilisation, they could gain a very competitive asset.

The embryo aircraft the Britannia team had set their heart on was the

Boeing 737–200 series. Although many airlines worldwide had historically expressed their faith in Boeing products, the company had been late coming into the shorthaul twin jet scene. While both Douglas and the British Aircraft Corporation, now British Aerospace, had been in the market with 'twins' for some time, Boeing had been handsomely scooping the pool with their three-engined 727 which, at one stage, became the world's top selling aircraft.

When they did take the decision to enter the two-engined market, Boeing's philosophy was to incorporate the same body cross-section as the Boeing 707 and 727, with six abreast seating. A controversial decision was to have the engines slung directly underneath the wing rather than the then more accepted practice, adopted by their Douglas and BAC rivals, at the rear of the fuselage. This caused a certain amount of comment because of the belief that engine ingestion from nosewheel debris could add expensive maintenance costs. Further developments, however, allowed the aircraft to operate even from unsealed airports.

Boeing decided to produce two versions of the 737, both to be powered by the Pratt & Whitney JT8-D which itself became the world's most successful commercial jet engine. The 100 series 737 got the production go-ahead on the strength of an order from Lufthansa for whom the aircraft was ideally suited with their intra-German network feeding into the Frankfurt international gateway airport. In parallel with this aircraft, Boeing were proposing a 200 series with a better range. This attracted United Airlines in the United States and it was this version that appealed to Britannia.

However, there were other outwardly competitive runners – and the Thomson directors were to become directly involved in the final choice in what Sir Gordon Brunton admits was "one of the most difficult decisions of my life".

The dilemma facing the Thomson hierarchy had several facets. The first was certainly those financial considerations. At a time when the group's debt equity ratio was one for one, they were being asked to commit multi-millions to heavy asset buying. As Sir Gordon wistfully remarked to Derek Davison: "If we find oil, you can have anything you want" (they did do so considerably later, with a North Sea 'gusher', and Davison was not slow to remind Brunton of his promise on more than one subsequent occasion).

Another distinct disadvantage was that the group still had little knowledge of the airline business on which to form a sound judgment. "We had not been around very long, and they still did not know us well," Davison points out.

And as though these were not enough managerial greasy poles, getting to grips was made more difficult by political intervention.

At the time the Luton men began to assess their jet options, just thirty odd miles to the south at the Weybridge, Surrey, headquarters of the then British Aircraft Corporation, managing director Sir George Edwards and his team confidently believed that they had the inclusive tour market virtually sewn-up with the existing 200/300/400 versions of their BAC One-Eleven twin-jet. They had launched the aircraft on an order from British United Airways and had since sold to Eagle Aviation and Court Line. They were undoubtedly flushed with success when news of the emergence of a 737 concept filtered through from the Boeing base at Seattle on the west coast of the United States.

John Prothero Thomas, now a director of British Caledonian Airways, was then sales engineering manager with BAC and he remembers the reaction there at the time. "The 737 specification was tremendously impressive – it was faster, bigger, cheaper to buy or fly, had a longer range, and more payload compared to either the One-Eleven or the DC-9. I think we had two views of this – if it was so bloody fantastic there was not much we were going to be able to do anyway, and, alternatively, if it was a bit of Boeing bull it would not work as predicted."

What had brought those views sharply into focus, however, was the news given to Prothero Thomas one morning, right out of the blue, that in just a few days Sir George Edwards and a top BAC team were to have a high level meeting with Britannia to make a full presentation on the One-Eleven.

"That was very bad news as we had done no work on the presentation – and we had very few details of what Britannia required," admits Prothero Thomas.

He remembers that all they could do in the time available was to take a normal One-Eleven presentation book and place it in a special cover with the hopeful legend: "BAC One-Eleven for Britannia Airways". The only additional information was a single sheet of paper giving the economics of longer length sectors which interested Britannia – to try and match Boeing's brochure seat-mile costs, six abreast seating had been adopted. This was *just* physically possible, and was planned by Channel Airways, a One-Eleven customer.

So immediately before Christmas, 1965, the BAC team, led by Sir George, went into the boardroom of Thomson House in London to be faced by a team headed by Gordon Brunton, Jed Williams and Britannia director Peter Swift.

"We were seated at the longest boardroom table I have ever seen," Prothero Thomas remembers. "Sir George said he did not want to waste time and immediately invited me to tell them about the One-Eleven. I virtually read from the presentation book, whereupon Jed Williams remarked that it was an extremely interesting talk, but he would like to know a little more about the economics of the aeroplane. When I gave him further details, including a payload of 92 passengers at six abreast, he re-iterated that they thought the 737 was really the right aeroplane for them."

After that, the BAC team were invited by the Thomson men to a Christmas lunch which turned out to be far from festive. The depressing atmosphere was heavy with foreboding for them.

Meanwhile, a growing synergy was developing between Luton and Seattle. The Britannia exercise was an interesting challenge to the Boeing team because it was the first time they had worked to the concepts and needs of a 100 per cent charter inclusive tour airline. Charter work in the United States normally consisted of missions such as taking a football team to Los Angeles in whatever aircraft happened to be available.

Richard W. Taylor, then actively involved with the 737 programme, but later to become Boeing's vice president in charge of government technical liaison, recalls that what was needed to suit Britannia was an extension of the fundamental design of the 737–200 aeroplane, particularly in the requirement for longer range. From a performance aspect, the airflow was improved, but they also had to study the passenger cabin to achieve more seats, more closets, and room to store the then unknown phenomenon in the United States – duty free goods.

It also involved a fundamental approach rarely adopted then but which has grown in importance in recent years, as Dick Taylor explains.

"Most airline people looked at the airplane's characteristics first before they studied the financial deal. That's changed a lot in the last five years. At that time, Derek Davison was certainly involved from the point of view of the aeroplane's operating characteristics – payload, range, how far it can go on fuel, runway length capability, maintenance – but the financial side was always important."

While all these parameters were being considered, the 737 programme, to use Taylor's words, "nearly died". The US Department of Defense cut back sharply and Boeing had to lay off thousands of workers.

It was the atmosphere to discontinue a drawing-board aircraft but, thankfully for the future of Boeing and Britannia, the programme survived.

Even so, there were undoubtedly still some concerns at Luton, despite their continuing close interest in the 737. Derek Davison enumerates three of them.

"The first was the fact that it was Boeing's first twin-jet and, in those days, the ability to predict performance was nothing like it is today. It might not turn out as right as we hoped.

"Another factor was the United Kingdom certification for the aircraft. Again in those days, Boeing were not prepared to take on board any risks associated with UK certification, and so all those costs were payable by Britannia.

"The third issue was that Boeing's guarantee of the 'mission capability' of the aeroplane was something like 80 per cent of the nominal figure which they placed on it. We wanted a capability of a thousand miles range carrying 117 passengers, and their guarantee was nowhere near that. The aircraft would not even make Palma, one of our main destinations from Luton, which is 800 miles. We wanted it to make Malaga, our other main holiday airport, which is 200 miles further south.

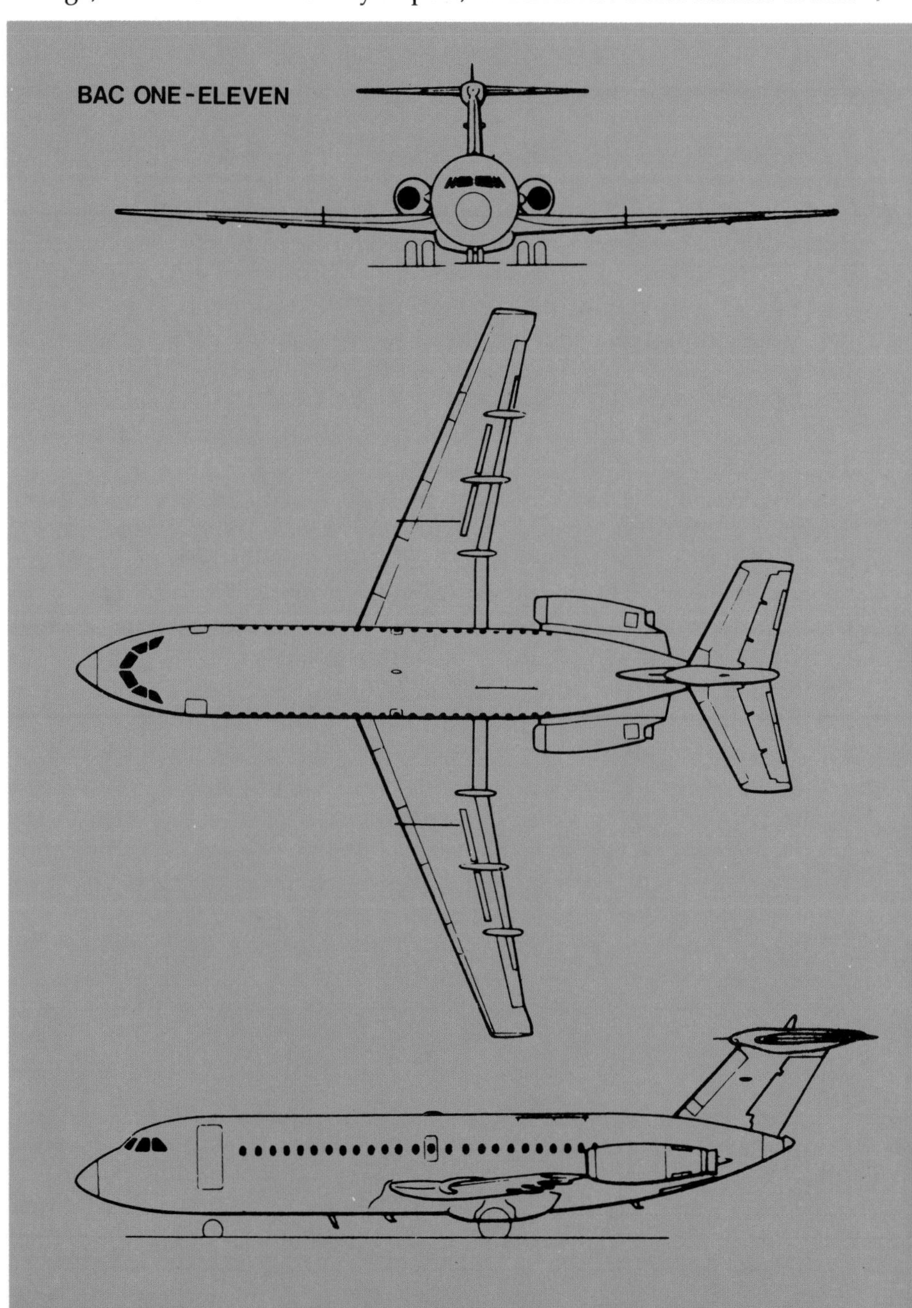

➤ *The aircraft acquisition choice facing the directors of Britannia Airways in 1965 was finally between the British Aircraft Corporation BAC One-Eleven and the Boeing 737.*

The nominal range would just about make Malaga, therefore our problem was to take a view of recognising the exposure which a company like Boeing would have in those days if they guaranteed something which did not come off. So they were going to be conservative about it, yet how much could we believe their nominal figures?

"The difficulty of predicting performance was such in those days, particularly with the new Boeing twin, that guaranteed performance contained a conservatism of around 20 per cent. The enhanced ability to predict today has narrowed that gap to two per cent on aircraft like the wide-bodied Boeing 767."

The Boeing 720, a modification of the more illustrious 707, had been introduced by Boeing for short to medium range operations but this was not considered competitive for Britannia's operations. The other potential competitor, the DC-9, had virtually been left in the stalls because Douglas failed to push its merits aggressively enough to the airline.

So there were now just two major runners left in the Britannia stakes. The infighting between BAC and Boeing became intense.

"George Edwards," says Williams, "was now fighting for his life. The trouble was that he had a bad case. There was just no way that, for

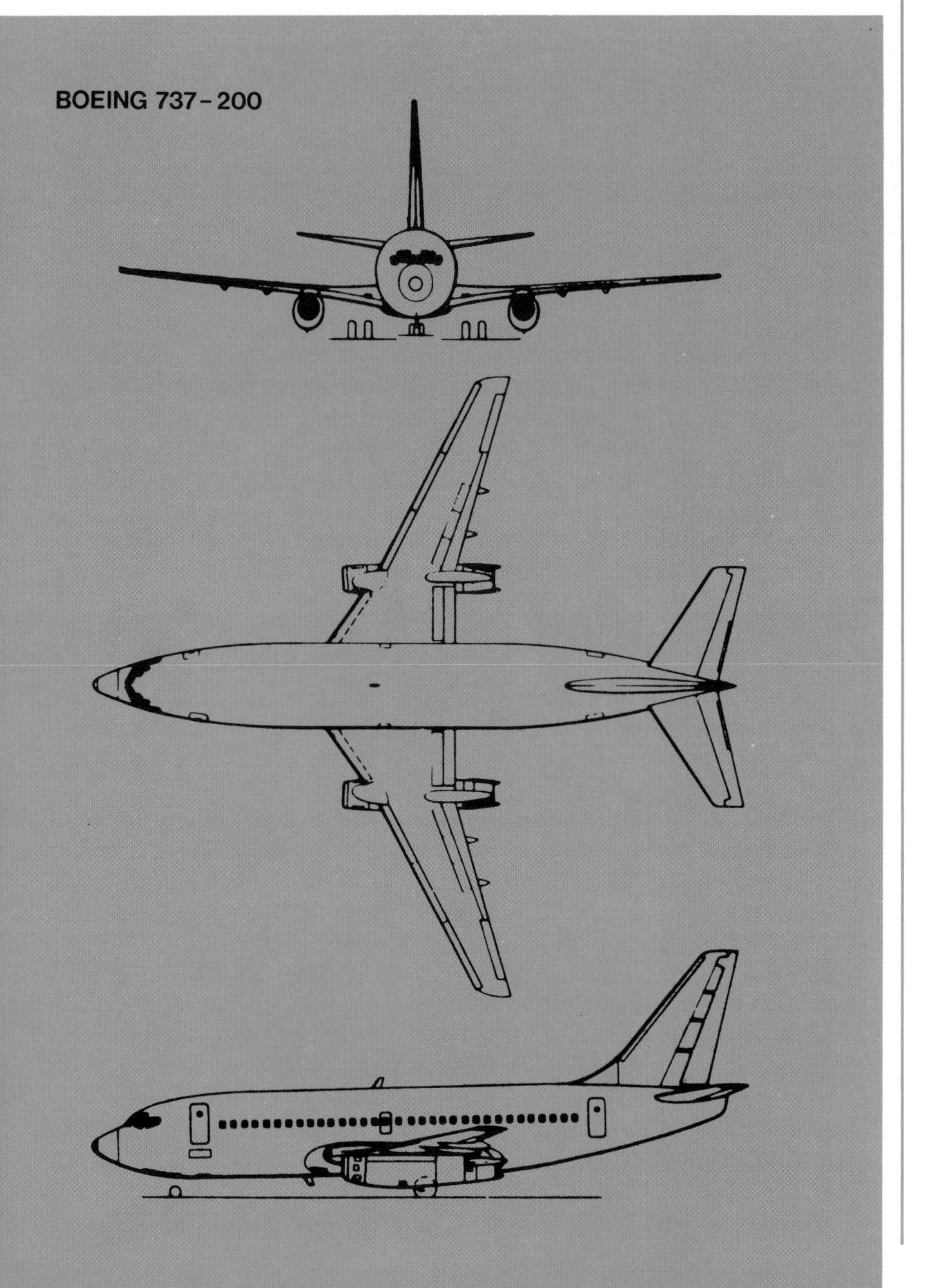

our purposes, you could compare the One-Eleven with the 737. It did not stand up on economics or performance – on everything you could name, the 737 was a better aircraft from our standpoint."

But the British horse suddenly took on a completely new stance when its rider decided to wear colours of red, white and blue. A hint of what was to come could, perhaps, have been seen in the reminder to Jed Williams by Sir George Edwards that, while British airlines had looked to the Americans for their long-range airliners, no British airline had ever bought a new short-range aircraft except from a British manufacturer.

BAC did not consider the cause lost. Sir George offered to stretch the One-Eleven, but then later he confided to Gordon Brunton that it could not be done. When Brunton told him, in that case, the Boeing would win, Sir George retorted: "If you buy the Boeing, I'll fight you all the way on the political level."

Soon afterwards, Tony Crosland, who was then President of the Board of Trade, was guest at a Thomson House lunch. Afterwards, Crosland asked to see Sir Gordon and Roy Thomson alone and told them what their patriotic duty was in the matter of buying their new aircraft. Not only that, he affirmed that, despite the fact that BOAC had been allowed to buy American aircraft without penalty, Britannia would be charged 14 per cent duty on every 737 they imported. The contention was that there was an equivalent British aircraft available, but Williams strongly maintained that, on efficiency grounds, that was not the case.

▲
Britannia's former chief stewardess Liz Harrison immediately falls for the contours of a 737 during a visit to the Boeing plant to see the first of the type being rolled out.

Too late for Britannia's purposes, BAC did develop the One-Eleven 500-B series whose undoubted merit earned it the distinction of becoming the widest-used European inclusive tour jet until Boeing produced further range capability into its 737s.

But, in addition to the new 'support the Union Jack' stand, Jed Williams' case was not helped when Gordon Brunton decided to get an independent view on the challengers for the order. He asked an aviation consultant, Stephen Wheatcroft, to evaluate the two aircraft. Wheatcroft strongly recommended going for the BAC One-Eleven. Despite that, and all the other pressures, Jed Williams described as "courageous" Brunton's decision to stick by the recommendations of his airline team.

The first time anyone outside learned of the final choice was at another luncheon in Thomson House. The guest of honour was the then Minister of Aviation, Roy Jenkins. Jed Williams was asked to give his views on the industry, and, introducing him, Lord Thomson added a sentence of five significant words: "We just bought the 737."

Jed Williams already knew of the decision because, a few days before the lunch, Roy Thomson had visited Luton for the first time. He listened to what was being said about the 737, then jammed his black Homburg hat on his head and walked out accompanied by Gordon Brunton. The next day the message that Williams received was even more succinct: "You're on!"

But still, as far as Britannia was concerned the UK government had to grant import permission for any Boeing 737 purchases. Therefore, although a contract was drawn up for three 737–200s, with an option on a fourth, approval was not received until June 1966, and even then there was to be no alleviation of the 14 per cent import duty.

Meanwhile, BAC had been given until February 1966 to come up with competitive proposals for the One-Eleven, but nothing substantial enough was forthcoming to persuade either Britannia or the government that the 737 was not the best equipment for the requirements.

When contacted by the press, Britannia claimed they had "bent over backwards to buy British", but after the months of negotiation, the BAC One-Eleven was economically unattractive when compared with the 737–200.

It is not difficult to see why Britannia bought Boeing. However far

▲
The fuselage of Britannia's first Boeing 737 being inspected at the manufacturer's Wichita, Kansas, site before being sent by rail to their Seattle production plant for final assembly.

they might have wished subsequently to support the case for re-equipping with the One-Eleven-500, the comparison with the Boeing 737-200 for the particular route requirements was heavily in favour of the American-built aircraft. Apart from any airframe considerations, one fundamental difference was that the Pratt & Whitney JT8-D engine in the 737 produced some 2000 pounds more thrust than the equivalent Spey in the One-Eleven, with only a slightly higher bare engine weight and about the same specific fuel consumption. This serious power shortfall arose from decisions taken long before, and it was not technically feasible to increase thrust in the Spey to compete in any sensible timescale.

Therefore, comparing the two aircraft, the take-off weight for the 737 was higher, which resulted in a maximum payload of 31931 pounds against 23430 pounds of the One-Eleven or, in terms of maximum range, 2080 statute miles against 1770. Maximum cruise speed was also appreciably higher while the balanced field length – the runway length required for take-off under the aviation safety rules – was marginally better. This was of considerable importance to Britannia operating from Luton where the runway is 7084 feet long – not over generous on a hot day. Subsequently the Boeing 737 has been developed through extensive airframe and engine improvements and the advantages are now even greater.

Romeo Lima, the airline's first 737, nearing completion at the Boeing plant in Seattle.

And, as Derek Davison confirms: "The choice we made in 1965 is one that we have never regretted. The 737 has proved to be extremely reliable in service, economic and flexible to operate, and popular with our pilots, engineers and passengers alike."

The way the Britannia team approached the task of making sure the aircraft was right for those three important classes of people did arouse a certain amount of curiosity and raised eyebrows at Boeing's headquarters. Normally, they are used to an airline sending a 20-strong team to Seattle who stay several months discussing the various aspects of their forthcoming fleet. They could not believe it when just three people turned up at 8.30 one morning – Jed Williams to talk contract points, Peter Swift, who had become 737 project manager, to have some engineering discussions, and Marianne Allen to choose interiors for the aircraft.

Jed Williams was asked by Boeing where his design team was. "She's here," he replied introducing Marianne who well remembers the occasion.

"The night before, Boeing had been very generous hosts and I had a hangover. They presented materials and pictures to me and then we had doughnuts and coffee. Normally, in those days, the fuss about aircraft interiors was unbelievable with discussions going on for months and months. The ten-man Boeing team could not understand that we had chosen our design in the course of that morning. Apart from the colour schemes, we had to choose the murals for the walls of the cabin. We had travelled out on Air India and they had pictures between the windows. We thought it would be nice to do the same with drawings depicting ancient forms of transport."

When Williams returned at 11.30am, Marianne told him what she had chosen, he approved, and the whole scheme was settled before lunch, as was the rest of the team's business. The Boeing executives readily accepted the Britannia attitude – by 4pm the same day they had prepared a huge card which showed how the design and materials chosen would look on the aircraft and presented it to the Britannia trio.

▲ *Now Romeo Lima is being prepared by Boeing for its delivery to Luton.*

Placing an order was one thing; finding the finance was quite another. That debt equity ratio of the Thomson business was, at that time, the worst in British industry, and to find the money was, in Sir Gordon Brunton's words, "a tremendous cultural shock". Although he says Roy Thomson was "marvellous" over the affair, there was just no money in the company to do the deal. In the end, finance for the first three aircraft was arranged through the Export-Import Bank of the United States. The rate was a highly competitive six per cent, but it did also need a guarantee from the International Thomson Organisation.

So now everybody at Luton was looking forward excitedly to the arrival of the airline's first new aircraft. But within a few months their anticipatory joy turned to intense grief over an incident involving their existing fleet.

In the early hours of September 1, 1966, Britannia Alpha November Bravo Bravo, with 110 passengers and seven crew aboard, crashed as it approached Ljubljana Airport in Yugoslavia. Only one stewardess and 21 passengers survived.

Reports indicated that the aircraft, flying a charter for Universal Sky Tours, was to the left and below the glide-path during its approach to the runway and, in the later stages, called for radar assistance. The weather was broken cloud with moonlight, despite the light mist.

The aircraft crashed in woodland, but there was no fire on impact. Unfortunately, as is the case in so many similar accidents, the inquiry found that the prime cause was the all-embracing 'pilot error' – so easily stated but so complicated when all the facts and the theories have been sifted. In those days, communications and systems were not so advanced as today when there is much greater monitoring of flights and navigational capability.

The accident was due to an incorrect altimeter setting, which, owing to the airfield's height of 973 feet, was so much more significant than if the airfield had been close to sea-level.

The vital change of altimeter setting takes place when making the approach and landing. Each airport has its own landing procedures so, on entering the airport control zone, the altimeter is reset for that particular airport. The pilot then flies the aircraft through the landing pattern to match the airport and a specific runway. It is this final change of altimeter datum which, though very straightforward in principle has nevertheless been carried out incorrectly by apparently responsible and well-trained crews on a number of well-documented occasions, with tragic results as in the case of Ljubljana.

Immediately they were told of the crash, Derek Davison flew out to Yugoslavia with a small team, and considerable activity also got underway at Luton headquarters. The tragedy also meant intense work at the airport itself. Air traffic controller Bob Easterbrook remembers being called by a reporter at 6.30am, making straight for the airport and then not leaving it for another forty-eight hours. Not only were there extra operational duties, but also hundreds of inquiries from relatives and friends of the passengers.

For Gordon Brunton, who was at that time chairman of Britannia Airways, the Ljubljana crash had at least one very poignant moment.

He had been on holiday in his boat off Majorca and when he returned to catch an aircraft at Palma Airport, he immediately saw the dejected appearance of all the Britannia staff there. It was only then that he learned of the tragedy. He flew to the site, arriving soon after dawn to find that the women of Ljubljana had spent all the previous night making Union Jack flags to place over the caskets containing the remains of the British passengers who had been killed.

There was also a positive sequel to the disaster. Brunton struck up a friendship with Dr Mirko Derganc, who was head of the small burns unit at the local hospital and whose team worked round the clock for two weeks treating the maimed. As a result the Thomson Organisation introduced scholarships whereby Yugoslav plastic surgery students were able to spend six months at a time in London to further their training. The company also donated equipment to Dr Derganc's hospital, and this was presented to them in Ljubljana by Derek Davison.

That incident was, fortunately, the only black spot in an otherwise distinguished career by the Bristol Britannias in the airline's service.

They lopped an hour off most of Britannia Airways' routes and were responsible, in 1965, for turning that budgeted profit given to Gordon Brunton of £180,000 into a magnificent £230,000. By 1966, with its all-Britannia fleet, the airline was claiming more productive capacity than any other wholly charter airline in the world outside the United States.

Into the jet age

CHAPTER EIGHT

Contrast in liveries. The Boeing 737 above, the first to be delivered to the airline, shows the livery which was later superseded by the red and blue scheme in the take-off sequence below.

It was after five hectic corporate rescue years as chairman of British Leyland that Sir Michael Edwardes asked himself the question: "Why go now?" His answer: "Because I can leave with an easy mind, a much stronger management team, and with more resources at their disposal."

It was the same time span from the formation of the airline for Jed Williams to be equally introspective. The acquisition of Britannia Airways by the Thomson Organisation had brought about a situation where he could give a broadly similar personal response to that of Michael Edwardes.

One milestone event had already taken place since the Thomson takeover. There is no doubt that Ted Langton was a one-off special – Jed Williams calls him a genius. But not only do geniuses not flourish in a corporate managerial setting, they positively wilt. There are scores of examples right from Henry Ford to Clive Sinclair. Langton was no exception.

Two years after Thomson moved in, Ted Langton moved out. Non-communicative to the end, he did not mention his imminent departure to Williams who was given the news over dinner by Gordon Brunton.

"Gordon and I saw the future of Thomson travel interests in the same way," Jed Williams recalls. "We agreed that the next task, as Britannia became increasingly important as an investment and profit centre, was to bring the airline more into the Thomson Organisation – to integrate Universal Sky Tours, and some lesser travel companies Thomson had bought, and to co-ordinate the product with Britannia."

But Jed Williams was also to become introspective. "At Luton there was now a strong team led by Derek Davison, financial director Bob Muckleston, and technical director Jimmy Little which did not need me. I doubted that one who had been a guerilla chieftain with Ted should commit the second half of his working life to being a staff officer in a proper army, however roseate its future and congenial the company. It was uniquely the proper moment to say so."

By now Davison had become operations director as well as chief pilot. There are many examples of very good airline captains who do not make

brilliant managers – it was the renowned ex-pilot Eddie Rickenbacker, builder of Eastern Airlines, who commented: "The trouble with these guys is that once they have had an airliner strapped to their ass for 10,000 hours they have forgotten how to think." Derek Davison was certainly not one of them, as Jed Williams confirms.

"Derek was quite exceptional. I have never seen another regular line captain come along the way he did. Pilots manage in the air without being creative, but in my organisation a line manager had to be very much self-contained and self-motivated. I expected line managers to be creative, and I did not want to hear about their problems unless they were insoluble."

Still only in his early forties, Davison was keen to keep flying and mastermind the introduction of the Boeing 737. But the inevitable question was who was to succeed to the managing directorship of an airline which had grown meteorically in half a decade and had been seen to have such high potential by Roy Thomson, one of the shrewdest judges of a business among public company chairmen?

John Sauvage took Britannia Airways into the next stage of its development when he became managing director in 1967.

The man chosen came from outside. John Sauvage was born in the Seychelles, but left the warmth of the Indian Ocean in 1939 to face the chill of wartime Britain. His service with the famous Pathfinder Group of Bomber Command earned him the Distinguished Service Order, the Distinguished Flying Cross and bar. Like so many ex-RAF pilots after the war, he gravitated into commercial flying. Sauvage took part in the Berlin Airlift, and then became chief pilot of Harold Bamberg's Eagle Aviation, swooping up the Eagle management tree to become operations director, chief executive and managing director.

When Sauvage decided in 1966 to begin looking around to further his career, the spectacular crash of what became British Eagle, owing creditors £5½ million, was still two years away. He had talked to Jed Williams and knew he wanted to ease out of Britannia and look to other challenges. Sir Miles Thomas was then on the Thomson board and Sauvage had met him in the days when he was chairman of the British Overseas Airways Corporation. He had two meetings with Thomas and Gordon Brunton.

They agreed that John Sauvage – one of the few real professionals in the independent aviation sector in those days, according to Williams – was the man to take Britannia into its next stage of development. So he arrived at Luton in February, 1967, at an airport where, 17 years earlier, he had taken off in an Avro York on the then grass runway for a flight to Hong Kong.

He recalls: "It was usual in those days to clear customs outbound and inbound at Bovingdon and re-position for Luton Airport in daylight – at least that was the normal practice, but occasionally the urgent commercial and maintenance requirements in between made it imperative for most, except the faint hearted, to attempt landings at night at Luton with the assistance of two rows of gooseneck flare perimeter lights – the mind boggles! I did not count myself amongst the latter, for being a chief pilot at the time I had to set a good or perhaps a bad example!

"I also recall the old Napier company's hangar at Luton with the lights full on and the hangar door wide open which did help on those occasions."

He was, however, immediately put under no illusions about having a philanthropic parent. When he suggested to Gordon Brunton, at the first board meeting he attended, that it was comforting to be working for an airline with solid financial backing, Brunton responded disarmingly: "You won't find it easy to get this organisation to part with more cash to buy more planes at three or so million dollars each!"

Sauvage inherited the eight Britannia 102s together, ostensibly, with the imminent arrival of the first of the brand new Boeing 737 jets already on order. But the second promised part of that inheritance became, instead, a baptismal headache.

Rumours began seeping through the mists of the Pacific west coast that Boeing were having problems with their 737 programme. These concerned both the structure and performance of the aircraft, demanding modifications to the wings. The need was to optimise lift and drag, even though the overall performance of the aircraft was exceeding the original expectation.

The short term result of all this was a delay in delivery of the first aircraft. For a scheduled operator, this news would have been unwelcome, but for a charter business which had pre-sold its summer flying programme for 1968, it could have been little short of disastrous. The answer was to lease aircraft to fill the gap. John Sauvage turned to Freddie Laker, and the result was a deal for two of Laker Airways' Bristol Britannia fleet. The blow was softened when Boeing agreed to pay for their short-term leasing.

So, instead of arriving in the spring as the herald of the seasonal inclusive tour programme, the first Boeing 737 – Golf-Alpha Victor Romeo Lima captained by Derek Davison – touched down at Luton from Seattle on July 8 right in the heat of summer schedules. Even so, after gaining

The two pilots who delivered the first 737 from the United States to Luton — Derek Davison (left) *and Don Tanton — also brought over the last of the short-haul fleet bought by the airline 15 years later and are seen here at the end of that flight. Below is the first delivery aircraft — G-AVRL.*

EVENING POST Tuesday, July 9, 1968

The pride of the puddle-jumpers

Feet firmly on the ground after their historic flight: Captain Davison, Mr Swift and Captain Tanton

jumps the biggest puddle of its life

THE PRIDE of the puddle-jumpers jumped the biggest puddle of its life yesterday — all the way from Labrador to Luton.

It was one of those things that they'll talk about in the Britannia Airways mess for years to come.

Boeing of America designed their 737 short-haul jet for trips of 1,200 miles at a time. But with a light load and the wind behind him, Captain Derek Davison, of Hitchin, stayed in the air for 2,700 miles — 300 miles farther than a 737 has ever flown before.

Captain Davison, 44-year-old chief pilot of Britannia, was delivering his airline's first jetliner from its birthplace at Seattle when he made his record Atlantic jump.

He made only two stops — at Montreal and Goose Bay — before flying the last leg non-stop and abandoning a planned refuelling stop at Reykjavik in Iceland.

He looked quietly pleased with his effort as he stepped on to the tarmac at Luton.

"A wonderful plane," was his opinion of the two-engined, 117-seater, registration number G-AVRL.

With him were Captain Donald Tanton and Mr Peter Swift, the men who have master-minded Britannia's switchover from turbo-props to jets.

Together they plan to bring a total of five Boeing 737s to Luton within the next year. The second will follow next month and the remaining three will arrive from America next Spring.

Cuts journey times

For Britannia, the whole fleet represents an investment of £8 million. But it will be "a very productive aircraft," say the airline chiefs.

Although it seats no more than the Britannia turbojets currently in service with the airline, it will cut journey times to Spain by a third.

And if it can come and go more often, it will earn a lot more money.

"It's the most economical short-haul plane per passenger-mile in the world, as far as we're concerned," said an airline spokesman.

Inside it looks like its big sister, the intercontinental Boeing 707, with six seats abreast. Only it has two engines instead of four, and is shorter.

But it can still make 550mph at 30,000 feet, and cruises normally at 500mph.

Gradually the jets will replace the fleet of Britannias which the airline bought from BOAC four years ago to replace its original fleet of Constellations.

Yesterday's 5½-hour marathon hop should reassure all the holidaymakers who will this year fly on the 737 to resorts in Spain and Majorca.

You won't have to worry about running out of fuel.

STORY — ALAN HAMILTON

PICTURE — PETER TITMUSS

The press gave extensive coverage to the arrival of the first Boeing 737 at Luton.

its certificate of airworthiness two days later as a new type on the British register, a VIP inaugural flight was arranged for July 22. Roy Thomson – by then Lord Thomson of Fleet – hosted 115 guests to Dubrovnik in Yugoslavia. The weather was so bad on the return to Luton the next day that Captain Don Tanton had to undertake two approaches before circling to make a successful landing. The commercial debut of the aircraft was a flight from Luton to Alicante.

The intensity of the flying programme, fortunately aided by the arrival in August of G-AVRM the second aircraft, was such that even deputy chief pilot Roy McDougall had great difficulty finding flying slots in order to convert to the type. He had, in fact, to carry out all his training at night. When an aircraft had finished its daytime work around midnight, often having been diverted to another airport because of fog before returning to Luton, he would take-off in the early hours with his instructor. This would be followed by a week of two flights a day to, say, Ibiza or Palma, by which time he was ready for 737 line command.

This was made possible because his boss, Derek Davison, had already qualified as an instructor. One of the qualifications was an instrument rating examination, but when Davison returned from his examining flight he was told by the instructor that he had failed because of a minor error. This was 7.30pm and, despite knowing that if he again failed he would be forced to wait some considerable time before being allowed to apply again, Captain Davison insisted he wanted to try straight away. He came through with flying colours.

Roy McDougall was filled with admiration. "I've always thought it was a very brave thing to do, particularly as he had gone through it once. I have always respected Derek for that."

They all found it was a considerable jump in technique to move from piston to jet engined aircraft. One aspect of the change was that pilots suddenly became aware they were eating much more quickly – so much so that Captain Don Tanton suggested they should not have meals at all on the aircraft. Unfortunately, that was not practical because there was not enough eating time on the ground at out-station turnrounds.

The Boeing flying instructors who accompanied that first delivery flight, in order to train more Britannia pilots on the 737, were obviously very conscious of the problems created by the change in tempo. At one stage Derek Davison had to reprimand them when he believed they were becoming too involved in the flight deck work. He demanded, "Look, you guys, I don't want people coming up here all the time. Don Tanton and I are delivering this aircraft, so just sit back and we'll get you there." The response from the passenger cabin was an outburst of cheering when the British coast was reached at Stornoway in the Outer Hebrides.

From that time, right up to the wide-bodied era, the Britannia Airways' fleet was expanded solely on the strength of this one type of aircraft, two of which had large freight doors fitted for the carriage of outsize loads. As Boeing and Pratt & Whitney improved the aircraft and engines with various modifications, the airline built in these improvements to the existing fleet, thus keeping abreast of the latest developments. The last 737 (G-BKHF) was delivered on March 23, 1983, also by Derek Davison, making a total of 31 new aircraft manufactured by Boeing to the Britannia specification.

The marked difference between the delivery flight of the first and last 737 clearly shows those appreciable advances. Romeo Lima had to refuel at Montreal and Goose Bay before reaching Luton via another stop at Prestwick, whereas Hotel Fox, 15 years later, made Goose Bay from

Below left *Two of Britannia's 737s have cargo doors. As the pictures below show, these are particularly useful for loading horses.*

Seattle before refuelling for the remaining flight to Luton. The in-service operational contrast was that the first aircraft was capable of 1,000 miles range with 117 passengers whereas the latest could carry 130 passengers nearly 2,000 miles.

As Derek Davison comments: "The development of the operational capability of the 737, both in performance and range terms, enabled the aeroplane to meet logistically the increasing requirements Britannia had for flying further afield to more southerly latitudes and from airports further north. The elastic was being pulled at both ends."

Boeing are the first to admit that this elasticity, allied to the performance of the 737 generally in the hands of Britannia, catapulted them into future orders for their airliner. Vice president Dick Taylor maintains that Britannia were a leader as far as the 737 was concerned.

"They were the first to get long hours out of the plane. We started to see the things we needed to improve the aircraft, and by incorporating them we both produced a better plane and reduced maintenance. Also we learned a lot from Britannia about improving despatch reliability of the aircraft – if they took 120 people out to the aeroplane, and it was not ready to go, because of their high utilisation they did not have another aircraft sitting around ready to call up."

So impressed was Dick Taylor with both performance and flight deck attitude of the Britannia team that, when there was a presidential commission in the United States into the advisability and safety of two-man cockpit manning, instead of the trio normal at the time for larger aircraft, Taylor asked three European airlines to give testimony. They were British Airways and Lufthansa, the two 737 scheduled operator leaders, and Britannia.

"The chairman of the commission was particularly taken with Derek Davison's candour on how they liked the aeroplane from piloting, training and safety aspects. I have no doubt that his testimony had a very great influence on the outcome of the commission's findings."

Britannia helped Boeing in another way by demonstrating the 737 to other potential customers. Following one visit to Sabena, both the Belgian airline's operations director and chief pilot told Derek Davison that the demonstration had convinced them that they had to buy the 737 for their fleet. At a later date, Britannia again demonstrated, on behalf of Boeing, a 737 to Maersk Air of Denmark at a difficult airfield in the Faroes. Maersk subsequently also bought 737s.

Chris Longridge, Boeing Commercial Airplane Company's vice president of marketing, readily testifies that co-operation of that kind "is ten

Vital to the in-service performance of the 737s was the high standard of the engineering. Here a team of Britannia engineers welcomes one of the early aircraft to their Luton base.

One of Britannia's 737s was, in 1980, named Jean Batten by the famous aviatrix herself. Superimposed on the picture of the aircraft in flight — G-BGYL — Jean Batten is seen with Britannia's first female pilot, First Officer Suzanne Eastbury.

times as powerful in the eyes of the customer as anything a Boeing guy can tell him." This was particularly so from an airline which was achieving the highest utilisation in the world for 737s – 4000 annual hours per aircraft. In fact, Britannia's 737 fleet has now achieved well over a million flying hours.

As Sir Gordon Brunton confirms: "A remarkable relationship was built up between Britannia and Boeing."

But at Britannia there was an urgent need for a relationship of a different kind – pilots to planes. Five 737s were to arrive at Luton within the first year of operating the type, and that demanded rapid training of sufficient flight-deck crew to fly them.

Don Tanton had been made chief training captain and the earliest conversions of pilots from Bristol Britannias had all to be undertaken in the air – before flight simulator training became available. This entailed 16 airborne hours for each pilot, but later use was made of a simulator being built for Aer Lingus, at a factory in Sussex, before it was delivered to Ireland. The simulator was still being used for conversion of Britannia's pilots after its installation at Shannon Airport and right through to delivery of the airline's own simulator at Luton in December, 1976, an improved version which has contributed to achieving an airborne conversion time of less than three hours.

One of the training captains in the early 737 conversion days was David Hopkins who joined the airline in 1967 from British European Airways and rose to become chief pilot, operations director, and managing director. Much of the flying training was then undertaken at Seville Airport because of the reliability of the Spanish weather and for its cost-effectiveness. But on one of these training sessions, cost and climate were not the problem for Hopkins.

He was in the middle of a conversion course with two pilots when spots began to develop on his body. As otherwise he felt fine, his two

Britannia managing director Dave Hopkins. He trained pilots converting to 737s at Seville in Spain.

◄ *Boeing 737s have achieved record hours with Britannia.*

pupils were happy for him to carry on with the timetable. But remembering his son had chicken pox at the time, it suddenly occurred to Hopkins that if the Spanish authorities saw the spots they might 'quarantine' him with a suspected infectious disease or force him to return to Britain. So he decided to hide in his hotel bedroom until any danger passed.

During the first years of 737 operations, there was another occasion when Dave Hopkins was apparently an unwelcome overseas visitor. In the early 70s, Britannia were undertaking a number of Far East charters with the aircraft to such destinations as Singapore, Kuala Lumpur and Hong Kong. Karachi was one of the staging points, and the Pakistani officials at the airport had a strong 'red tape' mentality, perhaps inherited from the British imperial civil service.

"On arriving there, I went to our handling agent to tell him to have the aircraft turned round, but he was adamant that our aeroplane had not yet landed. I tried to convince him otherwise, pointing out that I would not be there if it had not landed. As he had not been officially informed of the touchdown, he still refused to accept my word." Sometimes a bottle of Scotch or 200 cigarettes was a more telling argument.

India pointed up another example of the tribulations of the sub-continent. Landing in Bombay on one of those charters, Hopkins found the local ground engineers on strike, so the equipment for the turnround could not be provided. Hopkins and his crew decided to do the job themselves. Result: a 45-minute turnround instead of the normal Bombay time of one hour 15 minutes.

Around this time, British military trooping contracts to Germany had already begun. These have proved to be a useful revenue earner ever since, with about 17 flights a week bringing soldiers and their families on leave. They also provided useful sectors for pilot training. Later, a contract was also won for troop movements to Gibraltar.

Both the Far East charters and the trooping contracts were part of John Sauvage's double aim of not having too great a reliance on Thomson Holidays' business and trying to secure as much work as possible in the commercially hollow winter months:

"I was trying to achieve a balance and not to have too many eggs in one basket," says Sauvage. Yet the basket in question, Thomson Holidays, had been undergoing its own metamorphosis with a policy that was to hatch many more 'eggs' for Britannia Airways.

▲ *Not only are 737s used on trooping flights and regular holiday charters to Gibraltar, but Britannia also operates scheduled services on behalf of GB Airways.*

CHAPTER NINE

Touchdown in the west – and east

Companies are notorious for having their own 'Siberias' – the places and jobs where they put executives either because they want to forget about them or to test their mettle. Oil majors are prime examples, with highly forgettable outposts in Africa or the remoter regions of Asia.

It was the same with the Thomson Organisation in the late sixties after Gordon Brunton had taken the company into the travel business. In 1969, Brunton was looking for his fifth managing director of Thomson Travel within two years. The revolving Russian roulette chamber was pointed at Bryan Llewellyn who, in seven years with the group, had risen to chief marketing director of Thomson Regional Newspapers.

In this case, Brunton, though anxious to fill the post, thought, no doubt, that this would really test a high flyer then in his early forties. The background is explained by Sir Gordon: "We had seen our market share of holidays drop by half through competition from Clarksons, and we were being badly bruised indeed. We had not got our management right, and the only thing that kept the business afloat was Britannia Airways.

"I was invited to lunch by Hambros Bank who owned Clarksons. We were talking about the travel business and I remarked that the intense competition was ultimately going to end in disaster for some, with margins cut to the bone. The quality of holidays was declining, and we were all straining. I remember a very senior director of Hambros saying to me: 'The view we have here is that Thomson are basically monopoly newspaper operators and do not like highly competitive situations. Clarksons have taken your share of the market, and we believe we shall see you out.' I replied that they were mistaken and they wouldn't. 'If that is what you are basing your assumptions on, I can understand why you think that.' The following year Clarksons put their prices up because they thought they had the market – and we destroyed them."

The backdrop to that began when Brunton had shown equal conviction earlier in offering the travel position to his new protégé, as Bryan Llewellyn remembers:

"He sold the job to me as an exciting challenge and, as always in a corporation, one is inclined to accept the 'bull' that is given you without question. I certainly did not know enough about it to ask the right questions. That is how I got into it."

One of the first things he discovered was that the heads of the holiday company and Britannia Airways were hardly on speaking terms because of divergent views on the rates to be charged for airline seats. And the Thomson board viewpoint was that the travel business did not necessarily have to be the biggest to be the most profitable.

Clarksons, as the big operator at that time, were masterminded by Tom Gullick whose philosophy was to create more business by cutting frills and prices to the bone. When Llewellyn arrived on the scene, the 1970 Thomson summer brochure had been produced, so it gave him a breathing space to assess the market. By the spring of 1970 he was ready to go to Gordon Brunton and tell him, confidently, that the only way to go forward was to enter the price market, go for volume, and fight Clarksons head-on.

Llewellyn won his way, prices were chopped and the result was that he had the dubious honour of recording, in 1971, the biggest loss of any Thomson group company. But from then onwards, Thomson's share of the holiday market began to climb to such effect that, in 1975, after Clarksons had collapsed in the UK's then biggest ever travel bankruptcy,

Thomson Travel produced more than half of the Thomson Organisation's profits.

One vital element in this was the creation of the Thomson Holidays brand name, as the biggest in the business, instead of trading under a number of disparate entities such as Ted Langton's original Universal Sky Tours. But another was undoubtedly the relationship between the holiday business and Britannia Airways.

"John Sauvage and I got on together immediately because we saw eye to eye," says Bryan Llewellyn. "He needed aircraft utilisation and if we got the holiday prices right we would generate the volume. After we removed all the individual holiday brands we then owned, we marketed everything as Thomson Holidays and planned the best aircraft utilisation for them. We were after brand loyalty, and the 737s became part of the total holiday experience with their hot meals, bar prices, and duty frees.

"The holiday airline business, however, was a very different beast from the scheduled market. It existed on competitive charters drumming up business which, in some ways, was more difficult, but if you got it right it was much more profitable. The secret of getting it right was the extent to which you could increase utilisation of the aircraft by taking more work. Having done that you were then able to offer highly competitive rates which, in turn, meant that holidays could be planned at cheaper prices than ever before – which increased the utilisation.

"Of course, the per seat rates were less than the yield on a scheduled route, but if you are pumping 3,500 hours or more a year into a jet it makes a great deal of economic sense – costs were less per hour, overheads were reduced, and the only costs that did not reduce were the direct overheads such as flying the aeroplane. The more flying you do, the more you pay for fuel, you use more engine hours, you pay for more catering, but the costs associated with the support of the airline are greatly amortised.

Bryan Llewellyn who accepted the "exciting challenge" of becoming managing director of Thomson Travel.

"So we were able to offer, from that high utilisation, good commercial rates for the tour operation allied to an excellent aircraft in the 737 with its speed, comfort, very good reliability, and good catering and other cabin facilities."

The result was that from the first year in which the 737s were introduced, when the passengers carried was 463,000, the numbers nearly doubled the following year to 826,000. By 1971 they had passed the million mark at 1,266,000.

That year of 1971, however, was aided by a remarkable, though short-lived phenomenon which presented a long-haul opportunity in the United States. It demanded the speedy introduction of another aircraft type – the Boeing 707.

This was what became known as affinity group charters or, more crudely, the 'bent charter' market.

John Sauvage discovered a rapidly growing charter business for flying Americans, particularly from the West Coast, to Europe. To circumvent the rules which set a minimum price for travel across the Atlantic, intending passengers had to be affiliated members of a so-called club. It did not really matter what it was – Porcupine Club, Maiden Aunts' Club or Widgetmakers Club. The potential appeared so enormous that Britannia went into the market and leased one Boeing 707 from World Airlines for $6 million, and then another from Executive Jet Aviation.

The ex-World aircraft, now registered G-AYSI, also incidentally registered two 'firsts' when it arrived at Luton in February, 1971. It entered Britannia's newly constructed hangar and while there it was the first aircraft to receive the revised livery with a new red stripe to accompany the blue line along the fuselage, together with a modernised name and tail logo.

The inaugural flight of the 189 seater Boeing 707 in Britannia's colours was on April 27, 1971. Captain Roy McDougall took a party to Tenerife

The rapid development of charter flights to and from the United States required the introduction of a new type of aircraft into the fleet — the Boeing 707.

After the delivery of the first Boeing 707, the line-up shows (left to right): *Jimmie Little, John Sauvage, Derek Davison (all Britannia), Brian Cooke and Ed Daly (World Airways) and Peter Swift (Britannia).*

The crew who operated the inaugural flight of the 707 to Tenerife. It was captained by Roy McDougall (second left).

for the official opening of the Hotel Atlantic in Puerto de la Cruz. There Lord Thomson was able to tell his guests that Britannia was by then the second biggest independent airline in Britain having a turnover which would that year exceed £11½ million. "We are proud," he said, "of the service we have built up over the past decade and feel it compares very favourably with that of the State-owned schedule operators."

That trip must have given Roy Thomson a liking for those resort hotels in the sun, for afterwards he would occasionally travel incognito in the back of a Boeing 737, reading detective stories on his way to stay for a couple of days by himself in Tenerife, or sometimes in Majorca.

It was Captain McDougall who was to claim the unchallenged longest 'day' worked by any Britannia pilot in a 707. When the height lock on one of the aircraft's auto pilots would not work, the captain, Don Tanton, said he was not prepared to fly without it all the way from Luton to Los Angeles. McDougall told the captain he would be his human auto pilot. He rushed home, changed into uniform, and reported for duty to a somewhat surprised captain.

On the first leg to Los Angeles, they reached the Scottish border when a hostess reported she thought a passenger was dying. It was decided to divert back to Manchester and, with emergency steps and ambulance organised, they were on final approach to Ringway when a doctor on board diagnosed that the passenger was an epileptic and that he would be all right to continue. There was just time to do an overshoot of the runway.

Keflavik, in Iceland, was the first stop and, after refuelling, snow began falling heavily. Halfway down the runway, Captain Tanton could not see, so he aborted take-off. It was realised that with lights on, the glare obliterated visibility in the driving snow. The second try, without lights, was successful. Then after a five-hour wait on the ground in Los Angeles, the return leg was completed.

In all, Captain McDougall was out of bed for forty hours – but the assignment was perfectly legal. He was not a member of the operating crew . . . just a human auto pilot.

The 707 aircraft themselves were worked hard, too. The affinity group business was flourishing and, as a result, Britannia brought thousands of Americans to Europe. On one of John Sauvage's sales missions to the West Coast to drum up this business, Lord Thomson accompanied him to help sell the profitable charters.

The 707s were not, however, used just on these bonanza runs. Freight was a useful activity, two examples being a service between London Heathrow and Nairobi for Simbair, the cargo subsidiary of East African Airways, and the carrying of racehorses from Britain to Japan.

Sir Miles Thomas — later Lord Thomas of Remenham — was chairman of Britannia Airways when the intense pressure arose to end charters to the United States.

Although several of Britannia's pilots enjoyed their days with the 707 – Captain Jim Watret among them called it "a real man's aeroplane" – it turned out to be a short honeymoon. Political and competitive rumblings were beginning to be heard.

Airlines, led in the United Kingdom by BOAC, did not like what they regarded as a back-door method of undercutting their scheduled services across the Atlantic. One main victim of attempted lobbying was Sir Miles Thomas (later Lord Thomas of Remenham).

Though Gordon Brunton describes him as "a marvellous Britannia Airways chairman who loved the job and the staff loved him", he became the epicentre of the tremors which were reaching Richter-scale proportions. The pressure, however, was not confined to Thomas. It was equally applied to Bryan Llewelyn and John Sauvage, the official mouthpiece for the unease being the Civil Aviation Authority. As a result weeks were being spent by Britannia directors in hearings, and it became obvious that the wisest course was to abandon the affinity group charters.

As Sauvage had agreed wholeheartedly with the existing policy of not wishing to get into long-haul scheduled services, the two Boeing 707s were disposed of in the spring of 1973 to British Caledonian Airways.

There was no heart-rending wake at Luton as a result of the move. "As I recall it, when the decision was made," says Derek Davison, "we all felt some relief. This was partly because of the intense competition to all the gateway cities. Afterwards it became clear how right that decision was when the charter business on the North Atlantic simply collapsed."

As Davison reports, the aim was now to secure more aeroplanes and improve profitability. But within a matter of months of the ending of activity to the west, shattering news came from the east. The Organisation of Petroleum Exporting Countries, dominated by the Middle Eastern oil producers, had decided to raise their prices astronomically. In aircraft fuel terms it meant a trebling or quadrupling overnight of the 15 pence a gallon Britannia were then paying for their supplies. Surcharges had immediately to be imposed on the tour operators – not the best of marketing incentives because the value of the pound had also dropped so that potential customers were already feeling the economic draught.

A specific commercial tragedy of the OPEC crisis for Britannia was that they had just started developing winter holiday programmes. It was the beginning of the second holiday revolution whereby people who had bought a fortnight in summer were being enticed to take a short four or five day break to places like Majorca, for around £18 or £19, during the cold English winter. This was the brainchild of Bryan Llewelyn and, of course, was crucial in helping the winter utilisation of Britannia's aircraft. On the tour operating side in those days, even a one per cent increase in load factor boosted Thomson Holidays profits by a staggering amount.

But all that ambition was dashed by the news from OPEC. In fact, the following season, the inclusive tour market collapsed by 20 per cent. Meanwhile, however, the Britannia team had to come to grips with their own immediate over-capacity crisis caused by the holiday turndown.

Bryan Llewelyn told John Sauvage that he would have to dispose of some of his aircraft capacity. The choice was either to lease 737s to other operators – in a not particularly auspicious international climate – or aeroplanes would have to be sold. Sauvage managed to lease three of the aircraft to a Dutch company, Transavia, and another to Far East Air Transport of Taiwan, but a real breakthrough was created by the efforts of director Bob Muckleston and Derek Davison. As Llewelyn says: "They pulled the chestnuts out of the fire when it really got hot."

The Arab Republic of the Yemen covers just 75,000 square miles and has a population of less than seven million. But its geographical position is strategic within the Middle East – its waddied coastal strip fronts the south-east extremity of the Red Sea and its northern border nudges the desert heartland of Saudi Arabia. Its potential resources had yet to be properly developed, so the income of its inhabitants was among the lowest in the Middle East. For this reason, thousands of Yemenis in the seventies left for work elsewhere in the Arab world.

This traffic was one of the main platforms for growth of the country's airline, Yemen Airways, now known as Yemenia, who then wanted to enter the jet era instead of operating a piston-engined Douglas DC-6. This presented Britannia with the opportunity of leasing aircraft to the airline. The first to go, in December, 1973, was Romeo Lima, the first of the Boeing 737 fleet delivered to Britannia. Another 737 followed to the Yemen under what are called 'wet' leases – they are supplied with the full crew complement and ground support. Certainly those who took part have many memories of that interlude.

Though it was, perhaps, a small contract in overall airline terms, it was, admits Derek Davison, "a big deal in terms of worry". There was anxiety over safety because of the terrain and the state of the airfields.

"It was certainly a greater exposure than the normal airline operation," he confides.

This, in an operational sense, is confirmed by an experience of Captain

When the 1973 OPEC oil crisis hit Britannia, efforts to create new business resulted in a usefully profitable contract to operate two Boeing 737 aircraft for Yemen Airways.

André Jeziorski on his first flight to the Yemen from Luton. On the sector from Athens, Jeziorski was over Jeddah when he asked air traffic control at Yemen's capital, Sana'a, for the weather at the airport which is 8,000 feet above sea level. The controller said visibility was only 400 metres, so the 737 captain decided to divert to Jeddah. It turned out, in truth, that Sana'a's visibility was a clear ten kilometres – the air traffic controller had been fooled by a contractor creating dust from crushing stone close to the control tower.

One of the longest flights Jeziorski undertook from Sana'a was to Moscow – and the visibility there was certainly exceptional. The Russians insisted on having a Soviet navigator on the flight deck because they maintained Odessa control could not speak English. But the excitement of that trip for the Polish captain was to be flying at 35,000 feet, and, from 200 miles away, seeing the golden cupolas of Moscow shimmering on the horizon.

Captain Dave Hopkins, who also spent time in the Yemen, remembers a very different 'Soviet' story. He was walking along a road and a band of Yemeni approached him with the demanding question: "Are you Russian?" When he told them he wasn't, one of the men replied "Ruskies" and made a sign with his hands indicating a slitting of the throat.

Though the Yemeni contract exposed some of the younger pilots to the 'excitement' of overseas work – and, from Britannia's point of view perhaps got any craving for foreign assignments out of their system – it became obvious that the earlier decision to have monthly tours of duty there was becoming too much of a strain. These were later changed to one week only duties.

Departure procedures from Yemeni airports sometimes lacked sophistication.

One of the problems was international communication, and deputy chief pilot Roy McDougall, who was responsible for the logistics of the Yemeni contract, managed an ingenious solution. One of the stewardesses on the assignment married a Cable and Wireless employee in the Yemen. As a result, a system was worked out so that, with the three hour time difference, all messages for Luton from Sana'a would be telexed every day at 6pm arriving in McDougall's Luton office at three in the afternoon.

Though the Yemen assignment lasted right through to May, 1976, it was always realised at Luton that it had a limited life. The Yemenis had their own national ambitions and wished eventually to have their own pilots and engineers doing the job. But the contract was usefully profitable to Britannia for those 2½ years and provided valuable work at a critical period.

There was another similar opportunity later, when Britannia provided operational staff to Royal Brunei Airlines.

But if that year of 1976 saw the ending of a short era in the Yemen, it also heralded two significant events. The bold decision to go for further 737 fleet growth – and the appointment of Derek Davison as the third managing director of Britannia Airways when John Sauvage became head of Thomson Travel.

Sir Gordon Brunton looks upon Britannia Airways as one of the three best run companies in the whole of the Thomson Organisation. "It was true under Williams; it was true under Sauvage; and it is true under Davison."

So the man who flew that first lone Constellation into Luton fourteen years earlier was now to take the left-hand seat of an airline which had fourteen aircraft and was flying 2¼ million holidaymakers a year in a route pattern from the Canaries in the south to Scandinavia and Moscow in the north and to Rhodes in the east.

Just as Bryan Llewelyn had propelled Thomson Holidays on a trajectory for rapid growth, so Britannia Airways had set its course for improved profitability through the acquisition of more aeroplanes. Market leadership was the aim of both companies.

Britannia's expansion, of necessity, implied taking business from other airlines. Since Dan-Air was the largest airline providing lift for tour operators and other charterers, inevitably Britannia came to meet them head-on, and the two airlines changed position as market leaders in volume terms.

An acquisitive streak in Derek Davison came to the fore after he had become managing director in 1976 when he took a good look at Air Anglia, another then independent operator based in Norwich whose routes were particularly attractive to those engaged in North Sea oil and gas operations. As an example, they had scheduled services to Norway, and Davison felt that their passenger appeal could be boosted by substituting the existing piston-engined aircraft on those routes with Boeing 737 jets.

Negotiations got right to the stage of settling a price for the deal, but Davison claims that was the one and only occasion on which he was turned down by the parent Thomson board. They felt the take-over would represent a departure from the airline's mainstream business.

"I could see the force of their argument, but did not agree with them. I think we would have made a better job of it than what happened subsequently," he confesses.

Nevertheless, Derek Davison and his team were making such a good job of going for growth at Britannia that there was never any problem in persuading Gordon Brunton of the desirability of acquiring more 737s as and when they were needed by the airline.

"We were now commanding a great deal of respect from International Thomson in terms of believability and potential, and our customers were giving us confidence that we could generate utilisation on an increasing size of fleet. The pattern for seven or eight years was that we went along to ITOL explaining that we wanted another two or three aeroplanes. We always got the number of aircraft we asked for and, in return, I think we have done them quite well," said Derek Davison modestly.

But now there was to be a new chapter in aircraft acquisition. Undoubtedly the most momentous decision Davison would have to make as managing director, and ultimately as chairman and chief executive of Britannia Airways, was the choice of aircraft, and their introduction, to take the airline into the era of the big jets.

Britannia
SEATS
E143

Enter the 'heavies'

CHAPTER TEN

For insistence and persistence, the traders in the souks of the Middle East are reluctant introverts compared with the salesmen of the world's aircraft manufacturers. Their persuasive, even if more polite, ways are not surprising – they are not bargaining for a few dirhams or dinars; their ultimate prize could be an order running well into hundreds of millions of dollars.

Britannia's senior management had already experienced some of that in-fighting in the battle over the Boeing 737 order, but in the 13 years between that decision and the need to enhance the fleet again, the intensity of competition had grown in proportion to the size of aircraft. In the new era of wide-bodied aeroplanes, the narrow British competition to the Americans of the mid-sixties had now become the pan-European aerospace industry of the late seventies.

In the spring of 1979, business trends and a five-year forward projection indicated Britannia would need new aircraft by 1984. The Boeing 737 fleet was proving excellent value and eminently reliable, and although the company still had more of the aircraft on order, it would obviously not be competitively logical to go on buying the type for ever. After all, the 737 entered service in 1968 and, although its seat-mile cost economics were excellent, it would now have to be measured against not only the new, advanced members of the evolving Boeing family – the 757 and the 767 – but the competitors from McDonnell Douglas and Airbus Industrie, that new thrusting European challenger.

Boeing, by that time, had announced their 737-300 series. Fuel prices had risen significantly in 1974, and again in 1978. Technology had advanced in recognition, particularly in engine design. Advantages gained by stretching the fuselage to achieve extra seating capacity were diluted by a reduction in performance, and so the improved economics Britannia were seeking were not there.

Another stretched development of a popular aircraft, the McDonnell Douglas DC9-Super 80, was looked at, but it would have had a range of only 800 miles out of Luton and the target was 1,000 miles to reach the Mediterranean resorts which accounted for around half of Britannia's total business.

If the smaller sisters were not attractive, neither were the big brothers. The McDonnell Douglas DC-10 and the Lockheed TriStar were both considered to be too commercially penalising.

As Derek Davison comments: "Both those aeroplanes, with approximately 400 seats, produced the lowest seat-mile cost, but the utilisation we could get out of them was less than 2,500 hours, so the impact of that was actually to increase the seat-mile costs. The TriStar did not look as if it was going to continue in production, and the DC-10 had its image problem at the time, so we backed off acquiring these bigger, second hand airplanes." The Airbus A300 was also considered too big, with a similar impact on utilisation.

A direct Boeing 737 replacement would have been desirable, but it was obvious there was no such aviation animal. The exercise was not one involving a 737 replacement, but a displacement – was there an aircraft which could be introduced to displace the Boeing 737-200 on the airline's densest holiday routes?

Most of Britannia's tour operator clients had been telling them that they felt the need was for a 130-seat aeroplane – a similar capacity to the 737 – but with up-to-date technology. Not surprisingly, they also made it abundantly clear they did not want to pay more for their charters.

◄ Opposite *The Boeing 767 production line at Seattle on the west coast of the United States.*

Britannia's commercial director, however, inclined to the view that a configuration of up to 300 seats could be justified in the mid-eighties for the most popular routes. This view removed the hurdle associated with a larger aircraft. And so for the second time, Britannia were, as a charter airline, set to lead the way.

Underwriting this bullish outlook was an analysis of the effect on their biggest client, Thomson Holidays. The sister company put together a draft programme which showed they could already utilise two of this size aircraft in their following year's programme. In turn, Britannia themselves calculated that, for the year ahead, two bigger aircraft could be substituted for four 737s, without adversely affecting the complex dovetailing of holiday programmes. That this was acceptable in 1980 encouraged them in their fleet projections for four years later.

This requirement narrowed the prospects down to three – and those keen corporate salesmen to just two. Boeing had announced their narrow-bodied twin-engined 757, essentially produced for Eastern Airlines and British Airways, and capable of carrying up to 189 passengers, and the 767 wide-bodied twin medium range aircraft offering from 200 seats, with United Airlines as the lead customer. Across the Atlantic, a derivative of the A300 European Airbus – itself already eliminated from Britannia's studies – was the 210 passenger A310 which had gained Lufthansa and Swissair as initial customers.

The Airbus A310, one of the aircraft which was considered by Britannia for their new fleet.

The mouth-watering prospect for the men in Seattle and Toulouse was that an order from Britannia could swell a not over-endowed order book by at least $100 million.

In fact, Robert Ginns, project manager of Britannia's commercial division and the overall co-ordinator for the then new aircraft evaluation project, recalls that the managerial team decided they really ought to be aiming for a fleet of five new aircraft. These, they believed, should be introduced within a reasonably short period of time in order to spread the big investment necessary in training, tools, and test equipment as well as all the fixed costs associated with a move into a new breed of aircraft.

"We wanted to use the aircraft properly by getting high utilisation out of it and to be able to introduce a reasonable number of them in a short time. Though we saw the aircraft as a displacement for 737s, and that we would wait for a true 737 replacement, in the meantime we would be introducing a highly economic aeroplane. We would be replacing our assets but we would be maintaining the asset value and the profitability of the airline with this displacement fleet."

Following that first appraisal, which narrowed the choice down to the Boeing 757, 767 and Airbus A310, four committees were established to evaluate economics and performance, customer services, engineering, and flight operations. Initially, there was precious little hands-on material available – all three types were still 'paper' aircraft. Because of this, it was essential to ensure that like was being compared with like in the evaluation, as each of the aircraft obviously had very different specifications.

The staff responsible for the economics and performance report had, firstly, to study the specifications, particularly the weight breakdown. Each competitive aircraft obviously had different features to be taken into account – one would have a big door as standard, giving it the ability to carry engine modules, and another a pallet system in the cargo hold. So these peculiarities, together with major differences in the cabins, meant that various options had to be put into the mix in order to come up with a telling evaluation.

In this, Britannia did not simply accept the brochure specifications of the aircraft manufacturers. Bob Ginns and George Berrisford, who was Britannia's performance and navigation manager, flew to both the airframe manufacturers at Seattle and Toulouse. They wanted to ensure they were inputting the correct weights and specifications into the evaluation. They studied, for instance, take-off and landing performance. This was particularly important for Britannia which not only had to land its aircraft at holiday rather than international-standard airports in most instances, but also had a home base, Luton, which is 520 feet above sea-level and had runway length limitations. It was discovered that the specification of the 757 at that time meant there could have been need to reduce the payload in certain circumstances, and, in turn, the A310 was more limited than the 767, though not over the sector distances envisaged.

There have been detractors who criticised the 767 for its exceptionally wide 156-foot wingspan. This, they maintained, would create drag, and so affect performance. The obverse of the coin is that the wing assists airfield performance giving better lift, and also has distinct air traffic control advantages. The flight paths down through France to the Spanish Mediterranean destinations can be heavily congested in summer. Flying at altitudes of between 31,000 and 35,000 feet is usual for the majority of aircraft types. But the large wing gives the 767 the ability to climb to 43,000 feet, and so air traffic controllers can often give clearance to a 767 at the British departure airport through obtaining a flight 'slot' over France when lower altitudes over the Continent are saturated.

Another important consideration was what is known as 'block fuel and time'. This is the precise art of studying the fuel burnt right from start, through taxi-ing, take-off, cruising, descent, approach and landing at the destination airport. There can be major fuel cost differences over those various segments of a flight, and although the committee analysed the figures for 1,000, 1,500 and 1,750-mile sectors, the most critical for Britannia was 1,000 miles because of the distance to those southern Spain destinations.

Defending the A310, Airbus Industrie officials – though they conceded that the 767 was more economic at longer ranges – maintained that there was a cross-over point making the Airbus more fuel rewarding over shorter distances. Britannia judged it to be much lower than that claimed by Airbus and much lower than the key 1,000 nautical miles. A crucial fact was that the 767 produced a better fuel-burn performance per seat than the A310 on the majority of Britannia routes.

Chairman Derek Davison was the first man in the airline to fly a Boeing 767 when he went to Boeing Field in Seattle to try a Delta-owned aircraft for himself. After two hours of circuits, landings and simulated engine failures he expressed himself "very happy" with Boeing's latest product.

The full payload range was, of course, itself another critical area to evaluate. Britannia's team needed to consider not just the nominal performance indicated by the manual for the aircraft, but also the guaranteed performance being put forward by Boeing and Airbus Industrie. The same assurances had to be forthcoming in such areas as altitude capability and noise levels.

In the economics arena, the ground rules which Britannia had built up from their Boeing 737 experience were applied to the bigger aircraft. For their own operating environment, Britannia had to apply their own crew costs, handling charges, landing fees related to aircraft weight, and a host of other considerations, plus, of course, the price of the aircraft. To compare like with like, they even paper-fitted each aircraft with the same engines.

Customer services director Robert Parker-Eaton recalls that in his sphere of activity there were two main concerns – in-cabin layout and service, and ground handling and turnrounds. In both of these, the challenge was to achieve equal timing and efficiency with the 737 fleet, despite having an aircraft which would be half as big again and carry twice as many passengers.

Obviously to be economic in flying competitively-priced inclusive tour passengers, there is a need for a high density configuration, and this does not add to the ability to give efficient service in the cabin.

Because the Boeing 757 is a single-aisle aircraft, it was impossible to add an extra seat abreast. But with the 767 and the A310, having twin aisles, Britannia were keen to add an extra seat to the rows, making eight

8-ABREAST SEATING

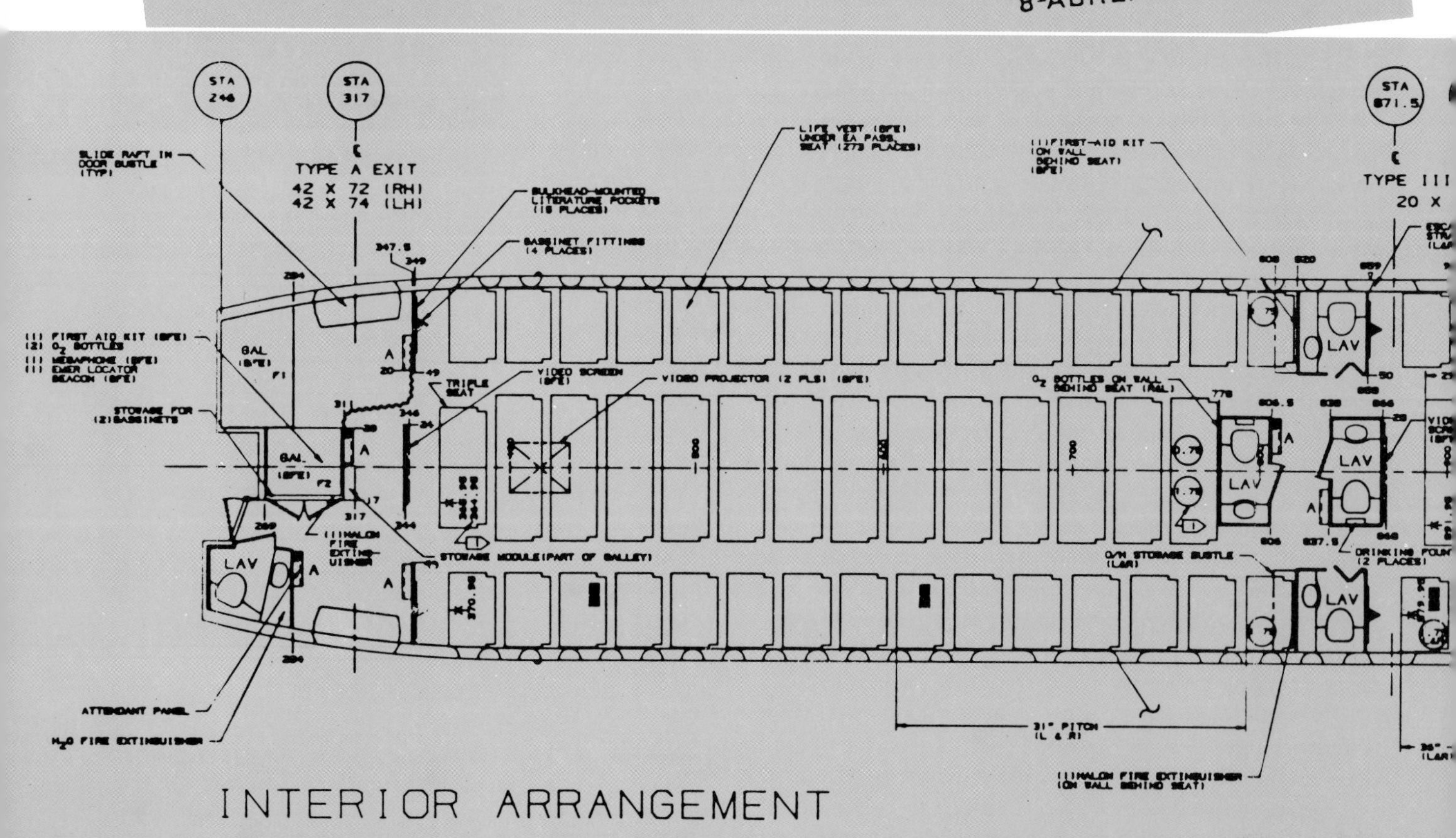

abreast in the case of the 767, and nine in the A310. Their decision was confirmed when later Hapag-Lloyd of Germany converted their A300 aircraft to nine-abreast seating and the bulky Germans among their holiday-maker passengers were quite content with the allotted seat space.

Another advantage of the 767 cabin which Britannia liked, as Boeing's then London-based chief Chris Longridge recalls, is the fact that it had constant seat rows with its 'rectangular' fuselage rather than the more cigar-shaped A310 which necessitates a reduction in the number of seats to a row at the rear of the aircraft, smaller galleys and offers no flexibility in the location of toilets.

The ability to increase the seats in two of the three choices, thus achieving improved seat-mile costs, was the first nail in the competitive coffin of the 757. Whereas the 757 would have had to remain at three seats either side of the central aisle, the 767 had the width to incorporate a seat configuration of two-four-two and the slightly wider A310 could accommodate three-three-three.

This meant about an extra 30 passengers could be flown in each type, though with an admittedly adverse trade-off of slightly narrower aisles. To compensate for this, the committee proposed an improvement in seat pitch allowing 31 inches instead of the 30 inches the airline specified in their Boeing 737s.

An analysis of seat-mile costs based on these changes, compared with the 2.66p achievable over 1,000 nautical mile sectors by a new 737-200, showed 2.55p for the 767, and 2.57p for the 757 and A310, even allowing for a later revised layout proposed by Airbus Industrie.

Before long, the 757 was beginning to stumble out of the race, owing, in the main, to the perceived attraction of the wide-bodied aircraft. British Airways had picked up a claim by Britannia that seat mile costs on the 767 were superior to the 757. BA felt this could not be true, assuming equal comfort levels for the passengers. The key was the impact on comfort of the 767 eight-abreast layout relative to the six-abreast 757. Britannia

Left *A cross-section drawing of the fuselage of the Boeing 767 showing how the eight-abreast seating was installed to meet the special needs of Britannia.*

Below *How the 273 passenger seats are positioned in the cabin, with the toilets placed centrally. This reduces congestion in the aisles and aids cabin service.*

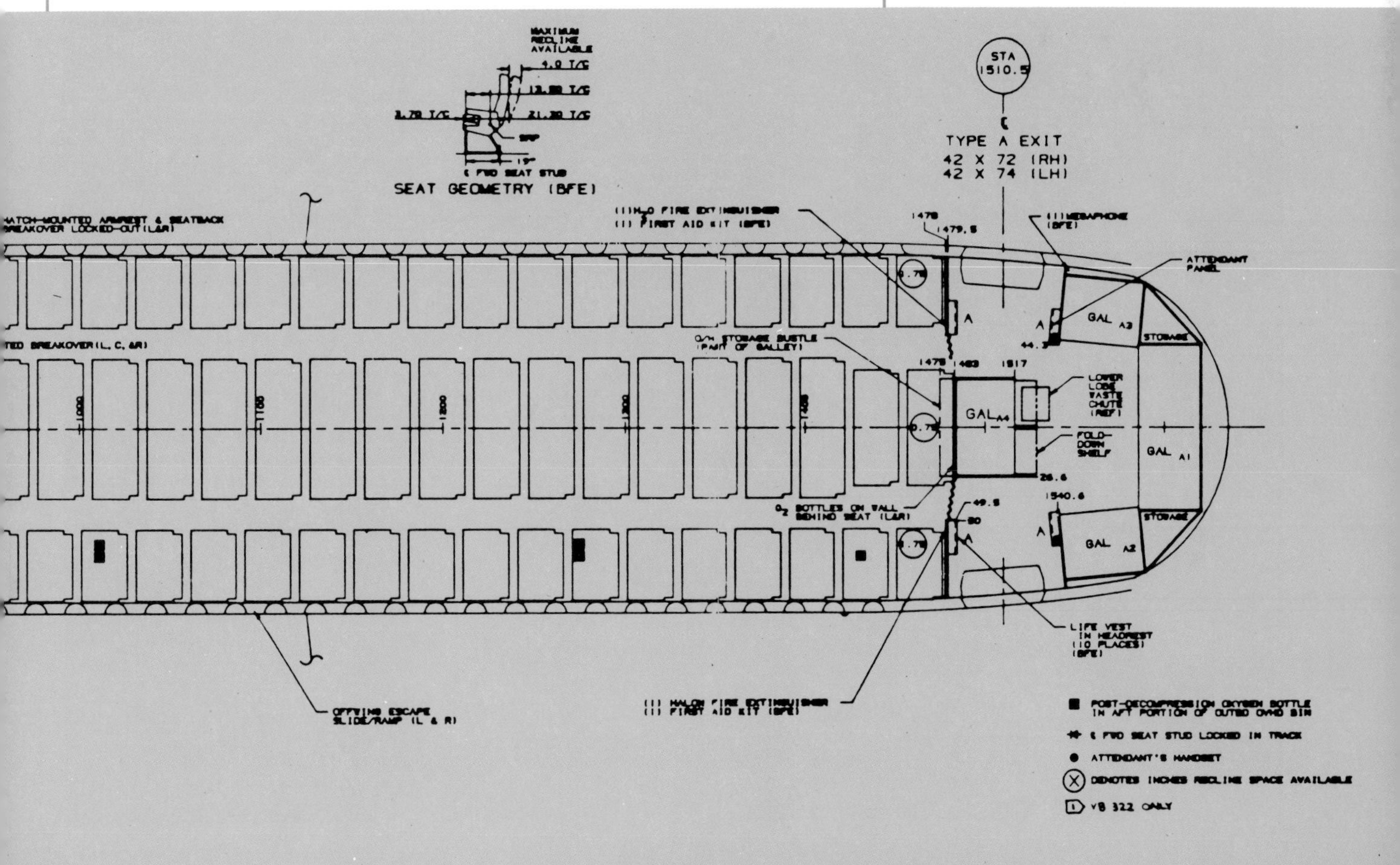

took the view that this was more than compensated by the twin-aisles, extra leg room and extra height. Britannia met BA, heard their arguments and were unconvinced. Nevertheless, it remained a worry, as it was to some extent subjective. "We now know we were correct in our analysis, and handsomely so," Derek Davison reports.

So now final negotiations were taking place between Davison and Tex Boullioun, president of the Boeing Commercial Airplane Company. Boullioun's personal presence at a London hotel meeting signified the importance he attached to the order, and the talks went on late into the night. After the meeting, both men went to a casino, and the Boeing president, a great gambler, was in his element playing three positions at the table with appreciable sums being waged on the turn of a card.

It was 3am by the time goodbyes were said – by which time Davison found that the gates of Hyde Park had been locked with his car inside. There was nothing for it but to drive across the park itself to get out.

By early December, 1979, firm proposals had been received at Britannia from Airbus and Boeing. This was on the basis of two actual orders, and three options with delivery of the first two aircraft in 1984, another the following year, and two in 1986. The proposals thus followed what had been a nine-months gestation period for the evaluation resulting in a study book of around a hundred pages.

It was a good Christmas, and end to 1979, for Boeing, although they were not then aware of it. For on New Year's Day, 1980, managing director Derek Davison submitted a recommendation, which subsequently received approval by Gordon Brunton and the ITOL board, for two 767 aircraft on the understanding that another three were to follow – a key factor as a fleet of two would hardly be viable.

Nevertheless, the final specification on which a contract was based entailed decisions on around a hundred different permutations for equipment and other 'add-ons' to the 767-200 series. These included necessities

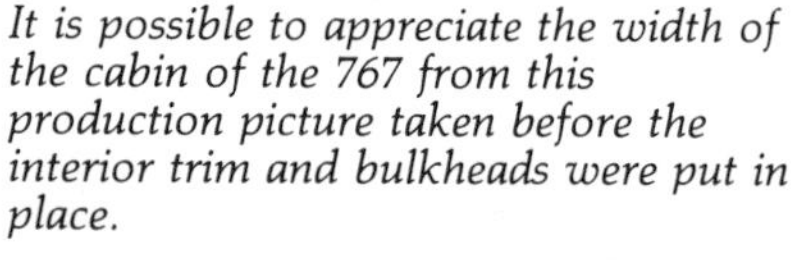

It is possible to appreciate the width of the cabin of the 767 from this production picture taken before the interior trim and bulkheads were put in place.

▲
Building a 767 at Boeing for Britannia.

associated with a high density layout, such as extra over-wing exits and extra seat rails (which Boeing offered free of charge).

As with a boy buying his first model train set, there were many other extras it would have been nice to have, but as Bob Ginns explains:

"We had to justify every item – either it paid for itself or we did not buy it. In theory, we wanted to purchase the standard Boeing aeroplane – everything extra had to be justified by the bottom line. We certainly did not buy anything for purely cosmetic effects. That would have been the worst of all reasons." Even so, the Britannia team felt the 767 had plenty of potential for future development through later specifications of the family.

By now, the men in Toulouse were beginning to spot ominous cumulus clouds coming their way from across the English Channel. They sensed there was an approaching storm which would sweep them out of the running. So much so that Bernard Lathière, the ebullient president of Airbus Industrie, flew into Luton for a personal talk with Derek Davison. A slight improvement in the offer was made which Davison believes Lathière thought was sufficient to ensure success. Unfortunately for him that was not so, as a gap of $3 million or so remained.

Yet even after the $100 million order had been announced for the first two Boeing 767s, the Europeans would not admit defeat. Bob Ginns took a call from Airbus Industrie's chief designer pleading that he could reduce the seat-mile costs of the A310 by stretching it and adding two extra rows of seats. Would Britannia be interested? Apart from the fact that no one at Luton could see how the re-design could be achieved successfully, the

Part of the negotiations by Britannia Airways for buying the Boeing 767 was for the manufacturer to take part in financing a simulator for training pilots.

economics still did not show any improvement over the Boeing choice.

A second round of negotiations now took place with Boeing, initiated by Britannia. The airline had liaised closely with Braathens SAFE in Norway, who were interested in the 767, over a common specification for the aircraft. Davison asked Boeing for a second negotiation based on this common specification and the double order. This resulted in a number of Boeing concessions to both companies, including participation in financing a simulator, which eliminated costs associated with the two pilot crew and the high density configuration.

Eventually, that original order for two Boeing 767–200s was to be doubled, another ordered for 1988 delivery, and an option still to be negotiated.

There was an amusing sequel to the order during the bi-annual Farnborough Air Show in 1982. Bob Ginns and George Berrisford were invited to the Boeing chalet, where Myron Anton, who was then Boeing's director of marketing for the 767, called to Berrisford: "Hey, hang on a minute, George. I've got a model for you in the back."

"Wow," exclaimed Berrisford, "is she wearing stockings and suspenders?"

Whereupon Anton reappeared with a splendid scale model of the victorious Boeing 767.

Models like this, together with detailed plans of the aircraft, had been studied intently at Britannia's Luton headquarters. There were urgent decisions to be made on the best cabin layout and baggage handling arrangements to suit the very specific needs of a high density charter airline.

Their advantage, as Roger Weeks who was then customer services' 767 project manager pointed out, was that they were starting with a clean sheet for a completely new aircraft. What they had to consider were the galleys, the galley equipment, the follow-on cabin service and every facet relating to where the passengers were seated.

Fundamental to galley equipment was the decision to opt for an off-the-shelf system called Atlas which had been developed in Europe and adopted by many scheduled airlines there. It is devised on a modular principle and is relatively cheap compared with tailor-made competitors. It is based on a series of slots which have the flexibility to take an oven, boxes, an aisle cart, or a combination of them. So successful was its adoption by Britannia and Braathens, that Boeing have now made provision to include the system in production-line 767s.

On all their aircraft so far, including the 737s, Britannia had served meals on hand-delivered individual trays. Now came the opportunity to move to carts, progressively parked down the aisles, from which cabin staff serve new-style meal boxes. The customer services team were particularly proud to have developed an ingenious letter-box type aperture in the front of those boxes so that, instead of having to take each tray off its shelf to place the hot dish on it from the oven, the cabin staff now simply feed the dish in from the front – a great time saver. So successful did the whole system become that the 737s have been partially converted to a cart service.

Time saving on the 767 was crucial. It was calculated that for a full 273 complement of passengers, an average flight allowed just 90 seconds to serve each passenger with a meal, drinks, duty frees, and attend to any other individual demand.

This narrow time-window meant that everything had to be done to ease the flow of service down the two aisles. Toilets are the big problem, because people walking towards them or queuing round them form human barriers to efficient service. The Britannia solution was to have the galleys at each end of the cabin, and the main toilets in the middle. The cabin crew are divided into two teams, each servicing up to the centre of the aircraft from the two extremes thus avoiding the jams around the lavatories.

Those toilets, incidentally, caused curious problems of their own in the early days of the 767. The lavatories are vacuum operated, their efficiency depending on a rapid swirl of water followed by a sudden whooshing noise as the clearing vacuum comes into play. The waste then passes down long pipes to holding tanks at the rear of the aircraft. In the early days of the aeroplane in United States service, there were complaints of disturbing clinking noises being heard all down the cabin. The phenomenon completely baffled investigating engineers until stewardesses were caught throwing away ice cubes down the pan. It was these that caused the noise as they rattled their way to the back of the aircraft.

So much for sewage, but it was the solution to disposing of rubbish of another kind that brought an ingenious solution incorporated into the Britannia cabin design.

As frequent flyers know only too well, aircraft cabins can quickly become airborne dustbins. Not only is the litter scattered by passengers objectionable, it is also a potential fire hazard. How to store it unobtrusively has always been a headache for airlines.

Bob Parker-Eaton came up with the answer. Below the rear galley floor is one of the 767's holds. Because of the nature of its traffic, Britannia always has excess cargo capacity, so if a hole could be cut through the floor of the galley it would be an ideal way of disposing of the rubbish below. Boeing studied the possibilities, together with an alternative of putting a lift into the aircraft – as is incorporated in the Lockheed TriStar – to give access to a 'below stairs' storage area, but this was not possible.

So the hole-in-the-floor idea was pursued, proved practical, and adopted. Now it is a highly-praised answer to the problem. The rubbish drops into a fire-proofed container which is carried on the multi-sectors of a flight and then emptied and replaced on arrival back at the home airport. It is also a positive step towards helping alleviate another perennial thorn in airline logistics – the short turnround time window.

To achieve Britannia's required 45 minutes turnround only leaves a 25 minutes cleaning and servicing slot because arriving and departing passengers account for the other twenty minutes when disembarking and embarking.

As Roger Weeks admits: "In turnround thinking, there was no point in copying anything an existing 767 operator or potential operator was doing because most of those customers were American airlines and there is a distinct difference between U.S. operations and those in the rest of the world." The Americans do not have the problems determined by inclusive tour configurations. The first buyers of the aircraft were scheduled carriers, and the airports in the United States generally had a higher degree of mechanical aids than most of the outstations used by Britannia.

So the old airline mnemonic to meet Britannia's needs was KISS – Keep it simple, stupid!

"That's what we really had to do," Roger Weeks reports. "We had to try and take into account Britannia Airways' need to put the maximum number of passengers into a sophisticated aeroplane. But the systems had to be unsophisticated compared with those for operators in the U.S. because we would be taking the aircraft to parts of the world less advanced like, for instance, Banjul in West Africa."

A difficulty was created by what Weeks claims is the only minus factor about the 767 – its fuselage shape compared to other wide-bodied aircraft. Its curvature means that the lower deck is not big enough to take standard baggage containers side by side. Introducing a special smaller container would have made Britannia an uncomfortable odd man out in Europe. So what was the answer? Standard equipment and simplified handling.

Overleaf *Boeing 767 in flight*

Britannia

BOEING 767
G-BKPW

A special loading procedure was therefore devised, utilising standard LD3 containers in the rear hold of the aircraft which would take the baggage for 250 or so of the 273 passengers. This took care of the bulk of the checked baggage.

The remaining suitcases, surfboards, wheelchairs and other bulky items are loaded into the front hold in a container designed for minimum handling by a small staff.

This has greatly aided quick turnround, as the majority of baggage can be despatched to the aircraft without waiting for the stragglers. All out-stations speedily got into the swing of the system – the only snag was when one particular new destination was introduced on to the network and, on the first three flights, the station forgot to unload the front-end 'bolthole'. Incidentally, the quickest full load turnround achieved was a staggering 28 minutes in Alicante, with Gerona and Banjul recording times only a minute or two slower.

The initial problem of inefficient use of the hold space for standard containers has been turned by Britannia to further advantage. By using containers with canvas sides, the spare hold space provided a walkway giving access to the containers which, when necessary, can be loaded or unloaded in situ. The aircraft can thus operate with containers through airfields lacking the necessary expensive container loading equipment. A strike of handlers at one airport, which caused other wide-bodied aircraft to be diverted because the baggage containers could not be loaded or off-loaded, did not affect Britannia's 767.

Crew baggage is another problem. Normally, Britannia cabin staff return to their home base the same day, but some rosters involve coming back to another UK airport, and so the crew must take overnight kit. With the height of the 767's fuselage from the ground, the cabin staff would not welcome their gear going into a hold, as retrieving it after duty would involve waiting for a baggage handler. Equally, passengers rightly become aggrieved if the storage locker above their seat row is filled with crew luggage when they attempt to place their hand baggage there.

Because the flight deck on a 767 is so spacious, Britannia believed that the area at the rear of the deck could just house a closet, which would contain all the crew baggage. Bob Parker-Eaton recalls Boeing's initial amusement when he first requested the stowage. So successful, however, has been this Britannia idea that Boeing now offer the closet as a standard option. A number of scheduled airlines use the facility as a wardrobe for first-class passengers.

If that item pleases the crew, 767 passengers are kept happy with another advance through the introduction of special in-flight entertainment. This is based on a multiplex system enabling all the commands for the entertainment programme to be sent down just one channel.

There are ten audio and two video tracks, but the novelty is that immediately after the emergency instructions on inbound flights, passengers are given a comprehensive review of the news they have missed at home during their fortnight's holiday. This is under an arrangement with Britain's Independent Television News, and the appearance of the news review is guaranteed to make passengers scramble for their headsets. These headsets, incidentally, are free, providing another saving in cabin crew time by obviating the need to tour the cabin collecting a fee. Perhaps the most surprised and delighted passengers were those flying from Tenerife and other airports on the evening of July 23, 1986, the very day when the Duke of York married Sarah Ferguson. There, on the screen, were the pictures of the wedding ceremony they had missed.

The fact that these passengers were sitting contentedly in their seats watching the Royal pageant emphasised the comfort of the 767 cabin. But both Derek Davison and Bob Parker-Eaton had one or two sleepless nights before the first aircraft was introduced. Would the eight abreast seating

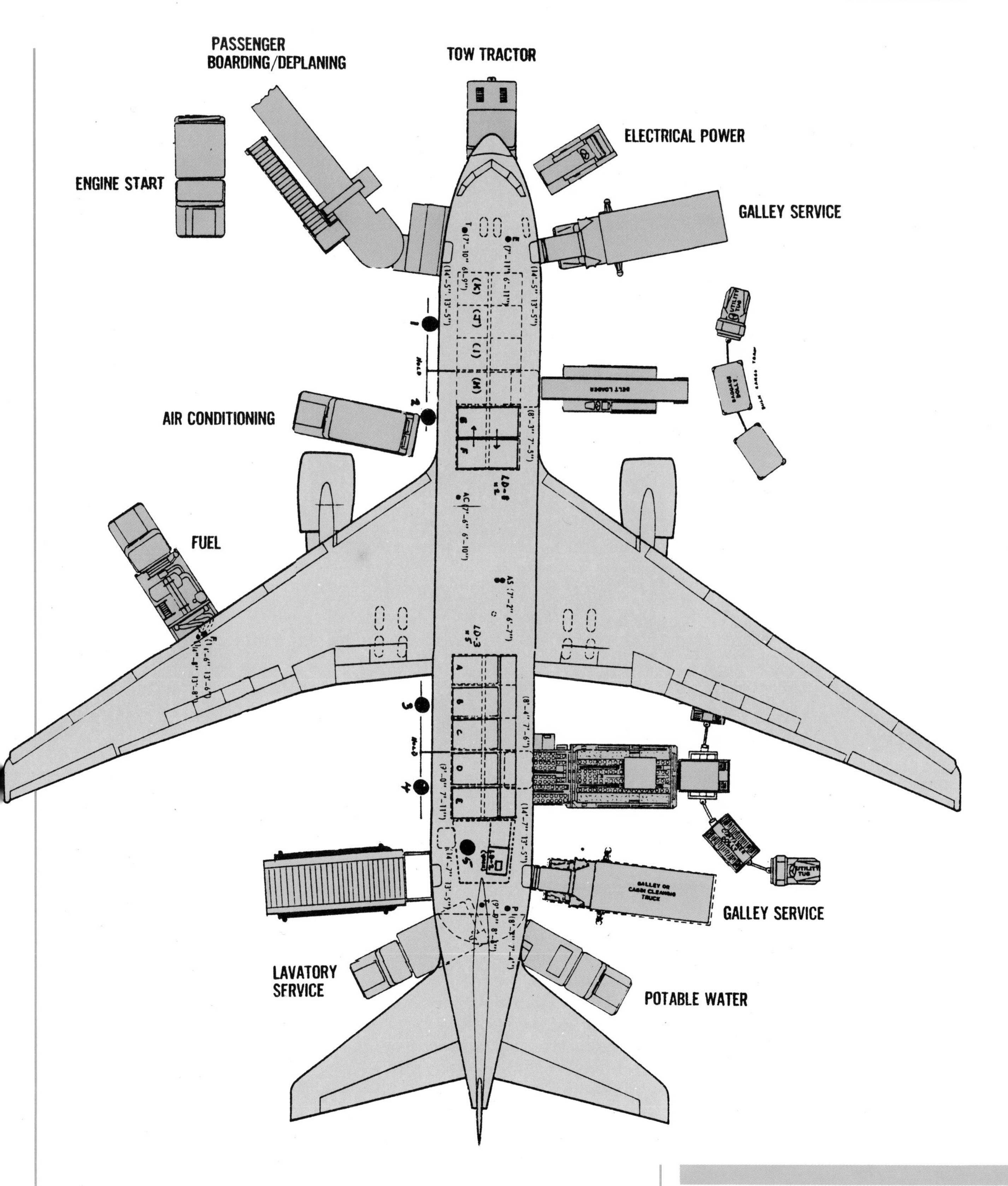

How a Boeing 767 is serviced on the ground. Britannia has to achieve a 45 minute turn round at out stations involving 273 passengers disembarking and the same number boarding.

The first airline identification for a Boeing 767 in the production plant is the rudder, seen here with part of Britannia's distinctive logo.

be acceptable? Parker-Eaton's worry became acute when, on a proving flight to Malaga just three days before the first commercial operation, disembarking staff commented to him "Oh, it's a very nice aeroplane, but the seats are too tight."

"Fortunately when we flew the first real passengers, they came off all smiles. Staff are notoriously the worst people to ask for an opinion," he says.

If the cabin crew developed a strong relationship with the attractions of the 767, it would be true to say that the men on the flight deck fell in love with it at first sight.

Stuart Grieve, who was the chief pilot and is now operations director, was invited with a few of his pilots to Seattle by Boeing to have hands-on experience of the aircraft some time before the first one on order was delivered to Luton.

"Although it was obviously a public relations job, we were all agreeably surprised, and I am bound to say, flattered, on how well we could fly the aeroplane. That spoke well of the design, because it was such an obviously easy aircraft to fly – and that is the way it has been in service. The blokes love it," Captain Grieve reports.

In fact, he says that virtually all the existing pilots who were certified for the 767 flew it better than they did the 737.

An interesting workload assessment between the two aircraft was carried out. Grieve and some of his fellow pilots had their heartrate measured while commanding each type. The parameters measured were take-off and departure, flying to 10,000 feet, and then coming in to land. It was found that on the 767, heartbeats were anything from 10 to 15 per cent less than on the 737.

▲ *Two Boeing 767s undergoing final preparations at Seattle ready for delivery to Britannia, and, below, Papa Whisky takes off for Luton.*

The reason for this more relaxed attitude was the advanced systems on the aircraft. Aids for navigation and flight-path control mean that, although it is a bigger aircraft than the 737, there is less to do on the flight deck – though there is more to monitor.

"If anything," admits Captain Grieve, "the concern is that the workload on the 767 is too low, which could lead to complacency and poor monitoring. Because the human being in general is a poor monitor, he can only monitor accurately for about five minutes and after that it is asking a lot of him."

It is, however, common knowledge that a pilot, after a lengthy trip at cruising altitude, gears himself up mentally and physically for the landing. This increases the arousal rate at approach and touchdown, yet even that was shown to be less for the 767. With automatic landings a pilot could simply press a few buttons and then just sit back and the aircraft would land on the centre line of the runway and carry on along it until it stopped. The only thing the pilot would then have to do is disconnect the auto-pilot so he could turn the aircraft off the runway.

Because of that, it is essential for a pilot to discipline himself immediately to be on guard should the auto-pilot malfunction.

The £4½ million 767 simulator, which Britannia bought in conjunction with Braathens, played a valuable part in this new learning curve. For the first time, Britannia had a simulator before the introduction of a new aircraft, with all the benefits in cost and time which accrue from that. The alternative – sending pilots to the U.S. for training – would have been a very costly exercise.

So realistic was the 'hands-on' capability of the simulator that all the pilots needed to do, after their 767 conversion course on it, was to fly the aircraft for about 45 minutes out of an airport such as Shannon in Ireland. They were then fully competent to fly passengers, though early sectors were in the company of a training captain.

Before the pilots were put through their conversion course, there was some natural apprehension, particularly among the older ones, that perhaps a new generation of flying techniques was better suited to a younger generation of men. Eyesight was one of the factors raised – would the older breed be able to distinguish the colours of the new visual displays, and how would the wearing of glasses affect night flying? In the final analysis, only one pilot was unable to grasp the new technology.

"All the others," reports Stu Grieve, "were surprised how the concept had come over so well and how easy flying the 767 really was. It had nothing to do with academic levels, being able to see colours, or any other imagined mumbo-jumbo."

A great addition to the pilot's confidence, when the weather is bad, is the inclusion on the 767 of what is known as Category III landing. This means that the aircraft can land at several of Britannia's departure and arrival airports when only 200 metres of runway are in visual range at a decision height of 50 feet. It was a matter of pride for 767 fleet captain Nick Pennington to receive full Category III authorisation from the Civil Aviation Authority in November, 1984, only nine months after taking delivery of the first aircraft – less time than any other operator had achieved with a new type of aircraft.

Chairman Derek Davison enthusiastically welcoming Victor Zulu to its future home at Luton Airport.

In fact, they gleefully relate the story around the Luton corridors of the day when a then well-known operator of Airbus A310 aircraft could not land at Gatwick and had to divert to Luton. At that time, the airline in question had not received Category III certification on the aircraft. The crew stayed at Luton overnight, but the next morning the weather had not improved. By good fortune, however, a Britannia 767 had to be ferried down to Gatwick and the marooned crew asked if they could hitch a lift. There was nobody more surprised than the controller in the Gatwick airline's operations room when his diverted captain informed him he would be landing soon.

"You can't land here – the visibility is still 250 metres," the worried controller told him.

"The fellow flying this aircraft thinks he can," was the reply.

All was later explained, and the 767 successfully landed at Gatwick by using a Category III approach.

There is no doubt that the Boeing 767's General Electric CF6-80 engines are a vital factor in the overall performance of the aircraft. The captain can monitor a wide range of engine parameters from the flight deck visual displays instead of, as in the 737, having to read cockpit gauges and write down the details.

The versatility of the power units means that take-offs can be undertaken with the engines slightly throttled back, which both increases engine life and reduces overall costs. The main element in the airline's decision, as Ned Billings, who was Britannia's engineering project manager for the 767, explains, was that they considered the CF6-80 engine had greater growth potential than its competitor. And they were also impressed with the product support being offered. In total, the GE package was superior to that of Pratt & Whitney. Derek Davison says: "We all sat round and the pros and cons of both engines were quantified into dollars. The resulting sums showed clearly that the GE engine, if the assumptions were correct, would cost Britannia less over future years. It will be a long time before we know if we got it right – but so far so good."

Below *Countess Mountbatten of Burma, with her sons Philip and Timothy, after the naming ceremony of Boeing 767 Papa Whisky 'Earl Mountbatten of Burma'.*

Below left *The Mountbattens perform the unveiling and, at the bottom of the aricraft steps, the Central Band of the Royal Air Force provided the background music.*

Below right *Inspecting a special display of engineering equipment on view in the hangar.*

The in-service figures show just how reliable those engines have proved to be. In the height of summer, they have a gruelling twelve hours a day usage. Yet despatch reliability – and Britannia use the yardstick of within five minutes of scheduled take-off time compared with the fifteen minutes allowance adopted by most other airlines – reached a highly commendable 99 per cent. In other words, only one in a hundred flights is delayed for more than five minutes for technical reasons.

Should there be an engine malfunction at an out-station down route, ideally a large cargo aircraft would be chartered and the engine changed in a very few hours. At worst, should this not be possible, Britannia's engineering department have developed sophisticated emergency techniques for dealing with it within their own resources.

The capability really goes back to the decision to opt for a modular engine. If the need is to replace a whole engine away from home base, then a replacement can be modularised into three sections and shipped out on pallets on one of Britannia's Boeing 737 freighters. That, of course, is assuming that the need is more serious than the simple replacement of one component module for the faulty one.

Britannia's engineers have equipped themselves with special tooling kits so that all that is needed at the out-station in question is a forklift truck and another lightweight truck. The engineers who travel with the replacement engine can do the rest. The whole mission should certainly be completed within 36 hours.

Fortunately, in the first year or two at least, there was no requirement to bring this rescue operation into force. This was in great part attributable to the computerised engine health monitoring programme introduced by the airline. Start-up, take-off and cruise performance for every flight are monitored, and then a detailed report is fed into a microcomputer system which analyses all the findings and provides a print-out. This is monitored by the technical support department, and if a trend is discerned – for example a gradual creeping up of exhaust gas temperatures – then they can call for a special check of the turbines or combustion chamber. So any problem is, hopefully, caught before it becomes serious involving, perhaps, only a simple module component change.

Stu Grieve is the first to acknowledge the benefit of the rapport which exists between the men on the flight deck and the engineers on the ground. Again that is another intangible Britannia asset handed down over the years. Alan Johnson, a familiar figure with his goatee beard, who was a line captain for two decades until his retirement in 1982, readily acknowledges: "A great deal of Britannia's success resulted from the co-operation between the crew and the engineering department."

Fortunately a technical problem on the delivery flight of the very first Boeing 767 to Luton was not an omen for the future.

As Victor Zulu was on its way from Seattle, a stewardess approached the seat where Britannia chairman Derek Davison was sitting and whispered in his ear: "Captain Hopkins would like to see you on the flight deck."

Davison hurried forward to find that the Boeing test pilot, also on board, had recommended the aircraft be turned round to make a landing in Montreal or, if necessary to return to Seattle. The chairman cleared the flight deck of all onlookers, apart from his two pilots and the Boeing test pilot whom he then quizzed. He found that there was a fuel booster pump problem. These pumps were only used as a back-up, but he knew the Montreal engineers were not going to be able to correct all four booster pumps. The Boeing man agreed there was no question of the malfunction affecting engine performance. Davison then pointed out that with Keflavik, Goose Bay and Prestwick airports available en route, there was no advantage in returning. By this time Dave Hopkins had already resumed

▲

The hangar in the background was specially built at Luton Airport to house the Boeing 767s.

◄

The crew who delivered the first Boeing 767 standing in front of the aircraft in the new hangar. Left to right: *Captain Dave Hopkins, Captain Eric Turner, and the 767 fleet captain Nick Pennington.*

the original easterly course, anticipating that his chairman's logic would win the day.

A fanfare of trumpeters from the RAF Central Band and a champagne reception were waiting to greet them at Luton Airport. There was no way Derek Davison intended missing that without an eminently justified cause.

The aircraft landed within a minute of the time set months before, ready for service, a tribute to both the manufacturer and the operator.

The Story in Pictures of a Typical Britanni

Britannia Airways' flight BY306A left Luton Airport for Faro, Portugal, taking 273 passengers to their holiday on the Algarve. These pictures tell the story of the flight, undertaken by Boeing 767 wide-bodied aircraft Victor Zulu, named Sir Winston Churchill.

1 *Passengers board Victor Zulu at Luton ready for an on-time departure.*
2 *The flight was captained by Dave Hopkins, Britannia's managing director, here taxi-ing the aircraft for a take-off from runway zero-eight.*
3 *The beginning of the bustle to achieve a 45-minute turnround at Faro. Aviation fuel is loaded to replace the 10½ tons used on the outward flight.*
4 *First Officer Barry Priest checks the intake under the wing.*
5 *Emptying the rear waste tanks.*
6 *Passengers' luggage leaves the hold in containers.*

Holiday Flight to the Sun

7 Dealing with the luggage stowed individually in the forward hold.
8 Meals go on board for the new load of 273 passengers returning to Luton after their holiday.
9 Captain Hopkins watches the loading of containers with the returning passengers' baggage.

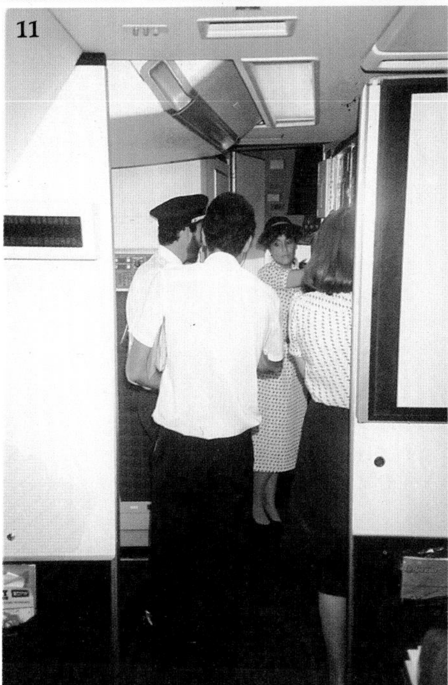

10 All checked, flight deck crew return to the aircraft for pre-departure routine.
11 Cabin crew give local agents the go-ahead to board the new passengers
12 Passengers arrive at the aircraft steps for flight BY306B which took them to Luton for on-schedule arrival.

CHAPTER ELEVEN

Password over the Pacific

Transmitting a secret password from an airliner flying over the Pacific Ocean would appear to be the scenario for a James Bond movie rather than the signal from a financial director for a business deal to go ahead. But, as we shall see, it was one of the stranger aspects of the complicated negotiations which are necessary these days when airlines order new aeroplanes.

The man in question was Peter Brown who had been recruited into Britannia Airways by chairman Derek Davison from the International Thomson Organisation where he had been working in head office following several years with the company's regional newspapers in the north-east of England.

By 1980, the annual turnover of Britannia was becoming large by any standards, having reached £150 million, and now the decision to bring Boeing 767s into the fleet involved assets then costing $41 million apiece. Davison reasoned that there was a need for a financial director with the competence to deal with issues of this magnitude to head the growing financial division.

Although financing, in principle, had been agreed for the first two 767s, much work remained to be done not only on that order but there was also the question of the follow-up aircraft.

Options had been taken for an additional three aircraft, yet before any could be converted into firm orders, the financing needed to be checked and re-checked and proposals had to be submitted to ITOL covering alternative financing arrangements and indicating the likely returns.

In a multi-national corporation such as ITOL, competition for investment funds is fierce. Major capital projects are subjected to the closest scrutiny and certain minimum criteria are laid down, principally concerned with return on investment, cash generation and earnings. Peter Brown thus found himself very quickly thrust into the big numbers game and before long was embroiled in detailed negotiations with the Export-Import Bank, the U.S. Government's lending arm.

Brown's long experience in the Thomson Group had taught him that major financial decisions could not be made by one company without considering overall group requirements, mainly the identification of the correct ownership vehicle at any given time. Britannia's interests, represented by the financial director, therefore lay not only in helping secure the best overall deal from Ex-Im but also in ensuring that its commercial position as airline and operator were protected in the wealth of complicated paperwork generated. The purchase and financing of the first 767, for example, gave rise to 29 separate agreements and associated sets of documents running in total to about a thousand pages. The negotiations with Ex-Im were not helped by their recent experience with Laker Airways whose demise had left the bank with second-hand DC-10s to dispose of.

Although not concerned with Britannia's status, which they recognised as blue chip with very strong backing from ITOL, Ex-Im's lawyers were nevertheless nervous and even more anxious than usual to dot every 'i' and cross every 't'. This proved extremely time consuming and, coupled with ITOL's complex ownership requirements, the negotiations lasted longer than had ever been anticipated. The final agreement was signed in Washington on February 7, 1984, the day before the first Boeing 767 was delivered.

After three years of negotiating with Ex-Im over the details surrounding the finance of the 767s, Peter Brown was the only director not present

Financial director Peter Brown: from newspapers to airlines.

at the arrival of the first aircraft – his flight back from Washington was touching down at Heathrow simultaneously with the 767, nearly 30 miles north at Luton Airport.

So the financing package was sewn up, providing availability of funds to cover most of the purchase price of five 767s. Ironically, after all the effort involved in putting together the deal, only one aircraft was financed by this route. Although the terms of the Ex-Im arrangement were favourable, they did involve direct ownership of the aircraft, and by 1984 it was becoming clear that ITOL's overall financial profile did not, at least for the time being, lend itself to this method of acquisition. The other choices open were to acquire the second aircraft by means of an 'operating lease' or to enter into a 'finance lease'.

With an operating lease, an airline pays a yearly rental for the length of the negotiated lease, usually five years or less, and then the aircraft returns to the lessor who has retained the equity in it. With a finance lease, however, the lease term is more closely related to the economic life of the aircraft, and the rentals paid by the lessee are calculated to repay the full cost of the aircraft. At the end of the lease period a sum equal to most of any residual value is refunded to the lessee by way of rental rebate.

The second route was one that Britannia had already taken successfully with some of their earlier Boeing 737 aircraft. As Peter Brown points out: "The choice of finance leasing for a number of our 737s has proved to be the right one. The aircraft have held their value remarkably well and our decision effectively to retain the risk of ownership has allowed us to enjoy the benefit of the high residual values as our early leases terminate. Had we been involved in operating leases, those residual values, which have proved to be much higher than for some other types of aircraft of that period, would have gone to the lessors."

As already mentioned, a pre-requisite to choosing the means of finance is the business justification for the actual acquisition of an aircraft.

Glasses are raised after the signing ceremony for the first Boeing 767. Round the table in Seattle, clockwise, *are Joe Sutter, at that time Boeing executive vice president, Britannia chairman and chief executive Derek Davison, Boeing's then London-based chief Chris Longridge, and Bob Brumage, Boeing's regional director, contracts, Europe.*

▲

Britannia's financial director Peter Brown (extreme left) *with International Thomson Organisation chief executive Sir Gordon Brunton* (centre) *and Britannia chairman Derek Davison* (second from the right) *and other members of the team who took part in the financing negotiations for the Boeing 767 purchase.*

Although the Britannia board had always believed that a fleet of at least five 767s would be required before the full benefits of the 'second type' would emerge, the current and projected commercial environment still had to be considered. Did the market and Britannia's share of it continue to justify investment in aircraft of this type, and would the return on investment meet the stringent demands of ITOL?

A detailed study by Brian Christian, Britannia's commercial director, was able to establish that future demand for aircraft seats would be sufficient to provide good utilisation for additional 767 aircraft at selling prices which appeared reasonable.

Taking these projections, Peter Brown and his team were then able to predict the cash flows and earnings from the aircraft operation. The critical point was whether or not these returns would be sufficient. The evaluation was taking place at the same time as ITOL was expanding its publishing interests in the United States, thus making competition for funds even greater. Nevertheless, Britannia's case was accepted and an order was placed for delivery of a third 767 in early 1985. At this time it was envisaged that the fourth aircraft would follow later, perhaps in 1986. This plan was changed abruptly when, in his 1984 Spring Budget, Chancellor of the Exchequer Nigel Lawson announced major changes in UK corporate taxation. His idea was to reduce the 'up front' tax advantages of capital investment while reducing the taxation on profits, and to achieve this he proposed the rapid phasing out of the existing 'first year' allowance. Between March 14, 1984, and April 1, 1985, the first year tax allowance available on plant and machinery, including new aircraft, was reduced from 100 per cent to nil and replaced by an annual 'writing down' allowance of 25 per cent.

On the night of the Chancellor's speech, Peter Brown, in common with many other financial directors around the country, was appraising the impact of the proposals. The third 767, already on order, was protected and would still attract the 100 per cent allowance. However, the fourth, scheduled for 1986 at the earliest, would receive relief on only 25 per cent in the first year.

The answer was clear. If two aircraft could be absorbed into the fleet before the end of March, 1984, then another order should be placed. Once again, Brian Christian did his projections, and a presentation to ITOL was made and accepted in record time. Boeing confirmed they could meet the required schedule, although the short lead time was almost unprecedented, and delivery would be very close to the fiscally demanded deadline.

The decision, already made in principle, to acquire one aircraft by a finance lease was extended to include the second 767, and soundings began with the financial institutions. It rapidly became clear that all the banks, through their leasing arms, were anxious to use up taxable capacity before the new legislation became fully effective. In consequence, when, in late 1984, a prospectus was sent to various leasing interests and banks, it generated considerable interest. Every one of the recipients responded with keen offers, the best, by a narrow margin, coming from Lombard Leasing, a subsidiary of the National Westminster Bank.

This offer was accepted in outline and detailed negotiations began. The clause-by-clause discussions went on virtually up to delivery date and involved several all-night working sessions. Parallel with this, a decision on the best ITOL company to use for the transaction was being worked on. The vote went to an offshore company which would enter into a finance lease with Lombard and then sub-lease the aircraft back to Britannia on an operating basis.

The timing of these negotiations was not so finely timed as those with Ex-Im, and were concluded with almost a full week remaining before delivery date.

Peter Brown was therefore able to compensate for missing the delivery of the first 767 by travelling to Seattle to participate in acceptance of the fourth. One further obstacle remained.

Boeing had its own financial planning team, and to avoid the imposition of a U.S. tax they required delivery to take place outside the State of Washington. So it was that Peter Brown, together with Derek Davison, found himself on March 25, 1985 departing from the Boeing field at Everett, not homebound to the east, but westbound over the Pacific to a precise bearing 46°54 north, 124°30 west where it was considered 'safe' for the transaction to be completed. A radio message back from Brown to Frank Bateman, Britannia's chief inspector waiting at Everett, the utterance by him of the magic password to the bank, and the deal was completed.

"Buying our new photo-composition machine at the Newcastle Chronicle and Journal was never like this," Peter Brown reflects.

Derek Davison signing the agreement to take delivery of the fourth 767 while the aircraft was being flown over the Pacific Ocean.

Chairman Derek Davison accepts the keys for one of the airline's 767s from Boeing chairman T. Wilson.

CHAPTER TWELVE

Fleet is dressed overall

Aeroplanes are like women – they must have the right curves to be attractive. But also, like women, airliners have to be 'dressed' properly to add that certain elegance to their original lines. Just as the great couturiers evolve their fashions to suit the times, so airlines have to keep the livery of their fleet under review, however much they may be sentimentally attached to their existing design.

So it was with Britannia at the beginning of the eighties.

When the airline started as Euravia in 1962, those first Constellations were painted in black, blue and white using what, in those days, was considered to be an elegant style.

In the early 1970s, with the application of that scheme to the Boeing 737s, partly because of the aircraft shape, partly because of changing attitudes to design, the 'look' was becoming old fashioned. Certainly, it did not suit the long Boeing 707s then joining the Britannia fleet. Elegance was abandoned for modernity, and a new red, white and blue livery with the complete logo of Britannia on the tail-plane was introduced. Within the airline the Britannia symbol was known, affectionately, as 'the old lady in her wheelchair'. It was under her steadfast symbolism that, for more than a decade, millions of holidaymakers had journeyed happily to the sun.

By the eighties, what had seemed ultra-modern at the beginning of the seventies was also becoming hackneyed. Not only had red, white and blue motifs been adopted by many other airlines, but the combination had permeated into other forms of transport. There were those at Britannia's Luton headquarters who were already beginning to wonder whether it was time for a new, bolder look at the livery when, coincidentally, the forthcoming arrival of the new wide-bodied Boeing 767s turned abstract thought into the need for positive action. When the existing livery was applied, in outline, to the wide-bodied shape of the 767, the effect was to say the least aesthetically anaemic. Something had to be done.

The Boeing company had an in-house design team which had historically created effective liveries for airlines and was willing to undertake similar work for Britannia. But there were two reasons why the Britannia livery challenge was not entrusted to the men in Seattle. The first was that, in the words of customer services director Bob Parker-Eaton who was responsible for masterminding the design input, "We felt the name Britannia has unique significance to the British – maybe old fashioned and emotional in some ways, but standing for quality, determination and honesty. Also, to our longer serving staff, the 'old lady' had a special symbolism. Our task was far more than merely being a design exercise. We felt only a British design team could properly capture that unique meaning."

So the search began for designers of vision and corporate nous. Though the design brief of the winner had to encompass everything from a sickbag to the Britannia logo now embellished in eight foot high lettering on the company's hangar at Luton International Airport, there could be little argument that it was still the livery of those aircraft that was the most crucial.

The search lasted a year and a half and covered the big and the small, but the choice fell to a smallish London design house called Peter Eaton and Partners. That 'partner' was an important element in the choice. John Piper had contributed to an earlier livery of British European Airways.

An essential ingredient in the production of a successful design scheme which Bob Parker-Eaton sought, in addition to flair, was an ability

The evolution of Britannia Airways' livery through the years. Left *The first aircraft colour scheme under its Britannia name was, in fact, adopted for its Bristol Britannia aircraft*

Below *The next colour scheme was to be seen on the Boeing 737s.*

Left *The Boeing 737 fleet was then given a much more striking red, white and blue livery*

Below *Today's livery evolved in conjunction with the dramatically different size and shape of the Boeing 767.*

The introduction of the present colour scheme was not confined to aircraft — it embraced the whole corporate appearance. A design standards manual was produced (right), and the illustrations on these pages are examples from the book of how the design should be used in a variety of applications.

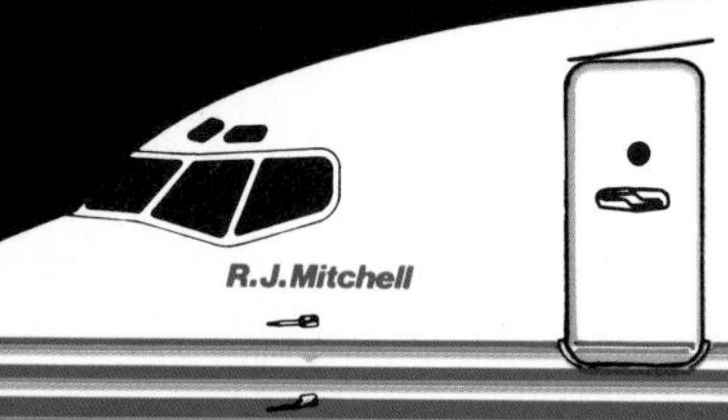

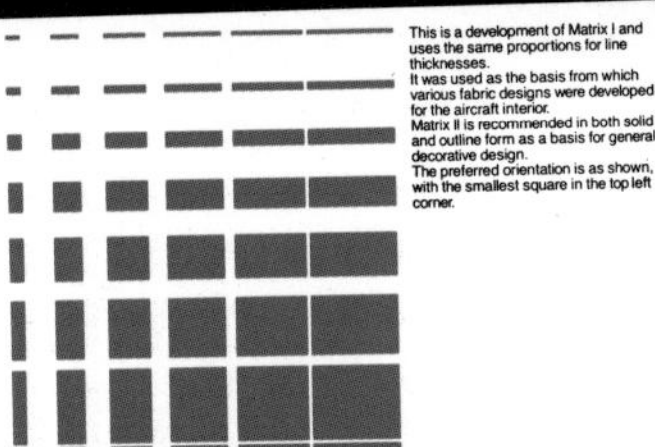

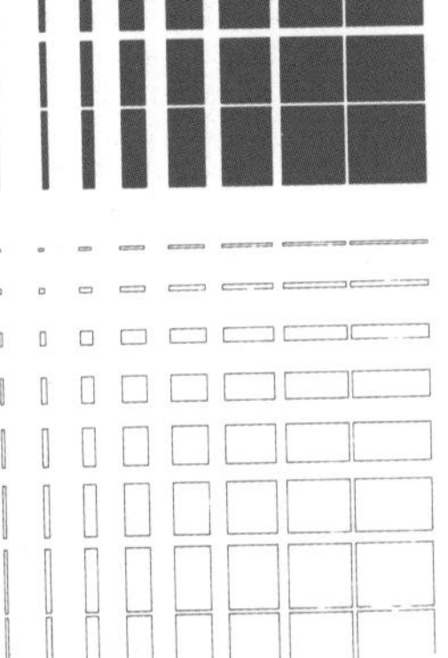

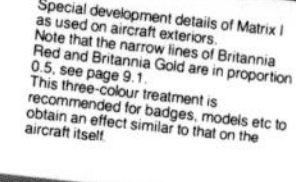

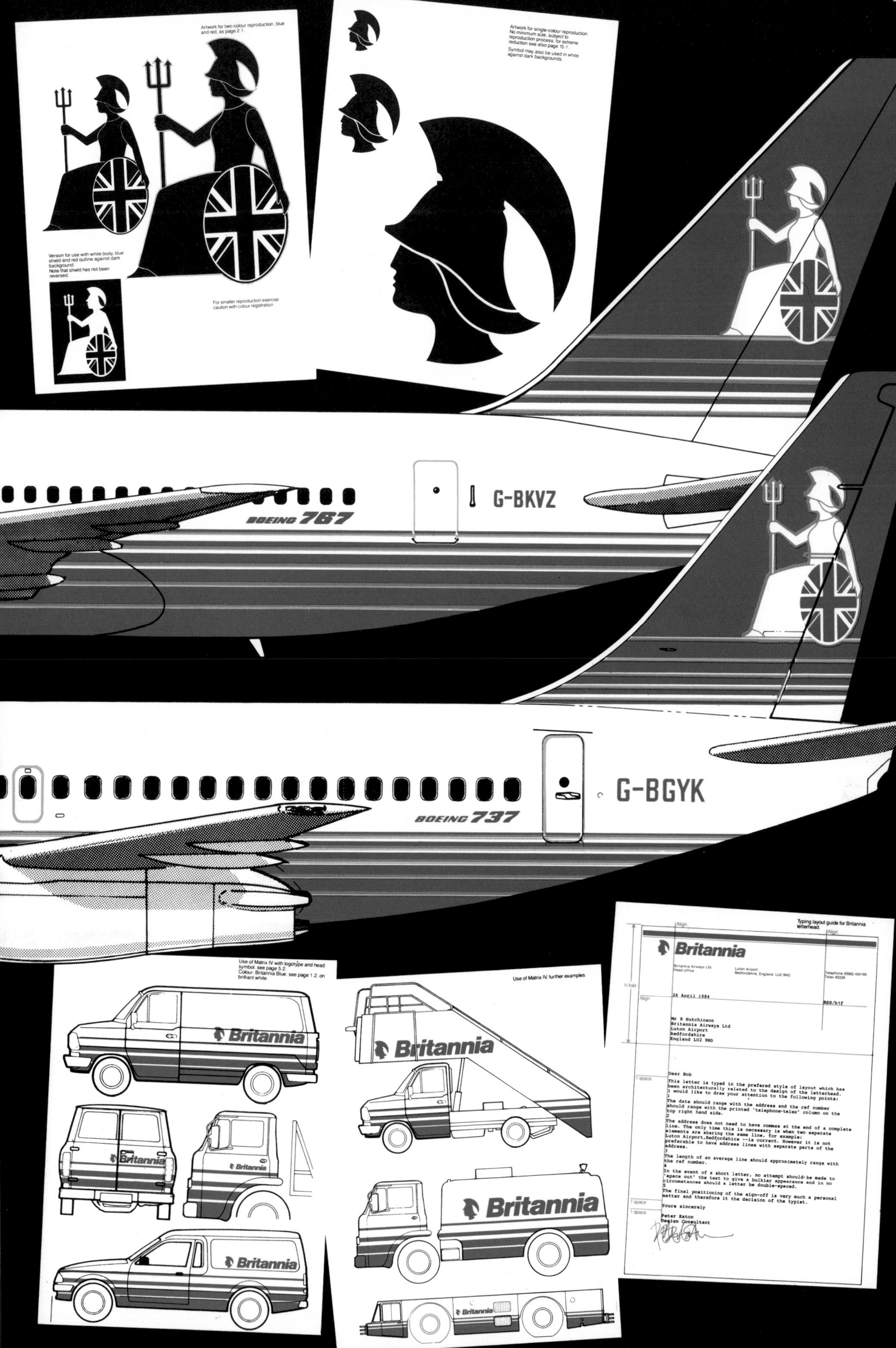

Britannia

Britannia Airways Ltd
Head office

Luton Airport,
Bedfordshire, England. LU2 9ND

Telephone (0582) 424155
Telex 82239

26 April 1984

RSH/hlf

Mr R Hutchinson
Britannia Airways Ltd
Luton Airport
Bedfordshire
England LU2 9ND

Dear Bob

This letter is typed in the prefered style of layout which has been architecturally related to the design of the letterhead. I would like to draw your attention to the following points:

1
The date should range with the address and the ref number should range with the printed 'telephone-telex' column on the top right hand side.

2
The address does not need to have commas at the end of a complete line. The only time this is necessary is when two separate elements are sharing the same line, for example:
Luton Airport,Bedfordshire --is correct. However it is not preferable to have address lines with separate parts of the address.

3
The length of an average line should approximately range with the ref number.

4
In the event of a short letter, no attempt should be made to 'space out' the text to give a bulkier appearance and in no circumstances should a letter be double-spaced.

5
The final positioning of the sign-off is very much a personal matter and therefore it the decision of the typist.

Yours sincerely

Peter Eaton
Design Consultant

The 'cheat' lines being applied to a Boeing 737

to relate to Britannia's engineers to ensure that the eventual design was practical as well as decorative. The then technical director, Geoff Parkins, and his engineering team had crucial inputs to make for the aircraft design to succeed. Their wholehearted involvement was essential. That experience and the personality of the two designers helped swing the day, and Peter Eaton and John Piper won the highly-prized design contract.

It was no easy task for the designers. As Peter Eaton diplomatically put it: "Britannia had strong ideas of what it wanted, and many concepts were eliminated as being interesting, but just not appropriate."

The 737 has always been regarded as a dumpy aircraft. The designers sought a design which would make it appear sleeker, at the same time one suiting the larger, longer 767. Stripes were used to achieve this.

Peter Eaton explains: "Stripes have existed on aircraft ever since they had windows. Early designers felt that windows were ugly and slowed down the eye, so they sought to create the opposite effect. That is why the lines were called 'cheat lines'. We felt we should give this idea a new presentation."

The designers had been working with Britannia's then colours of red, white and blue, without achieving a breakthrough. One day Peter Eaton casually commented how, paradoxically, Britannia's earlier livery of blue and white was now less dated in design terms than the present, newer, red, white and blue scheme. Derek Davison had always liked the old scheme. "Well, why not drop the red?" he said. And for good measure, added "Blue and gold, with the white would look very elegant."

That chance discussion was the catalyst. The elusive hunt was nearly over. A graded striping of horizontal lines was developed. However, although attractive, the design still looked somewhat cold and clinical. So Peter Eaton added back thin red lines between the blue and gold. The effect was magic.

Perhaps that magic had something to do with the date. For it was on Christmas Eve, 1981, when Peter Eaton and John Piper presented their final designs to the full Britannia board at Luton – and held their breath. After a long pause, Derek Davison looked up, smiling, and said: "We gave you a tough task, and a very hard time, but you have cracked it. That's our new livery!"

From that difficult start, the livery was translated to the aircraft interiors, airline vehicles, check-in desks, signs, stationery and the thousand and one other items bearing the Britannia name or logo.

The reaction of Dick Bernard, of Boeing's marketing team, was that the new livery had lifted the design level of airline corporate identity. "Its individuality is so striking that it will be a hard act to follow," he added.

Since 1981, airlines around the world have updated their liveries. It says much for Peter Eaton's design that, in the congested airfields of Europe, Britannia's aircraft still stand out in their elegant individuality.

Slight political and bureaucratic turbulence

CHAPTER THIRTEEN

It is no secret that, through the years, ministers and civil servants responsible for aviation in Britain did not have an overwhelming consciousness of Britannia Airways within their day-to-day activities. One bureaucrat who served in the department recalls that when he asked for the file on Britannia it contained little apart from an annual report, a few sheets of paper, and dust.

Perhaps the first minister to come to appreciate Britannia's place in the UK civil aviation scene was Iain Sproat, who, until losing his House of Commons seat in the general election of 1983, was, as parliamentary secretary at the Department of Trade and Industry, one of Prime Minister Margaret Thatcher's more promising eaglets.

"One of the first times that Britannia impinged on my consciousness was after I had spent a lot of time dealing specifically with the affairs of British Airways and British Caledonian. I was then surprised to find that Britannia was bigger than every other UK airline apart from British Airways." The airline blipped ever larger on Sproat's ministerial radar screen when one of his aides commented that, in his view, Britannia was also easily the most efficient airline in the country.

There is no doubt that a big part of Mrs Thatcher's admiration for Sproat was that, as minister responsible for aviation, he displayed a get-up and go attitude. He was also more than willing to shake things up to such a degree that the resulting effervescence often left indelible stains on

The then Aviation Minister, Iain Sproat, opening Britannia Airways' new administration building at Luton in 1982, watched by chairman Derek Davison.

Former Secretary of State for Transport Nicholas Ridley, accompanied by Derek Davison, at the naming ceremony of Boeing 767 G-BKVZ which became Sir Winston Churchill.

those in the way. Since his arrival at the ministry he had, perhaps subconsciously, been looking for an excuse to mix a potion. He believed it was not just departmental attitudes that needed a shake, but also bodies associated with his ministry like the Civil Aviation Authority.

In Britannia, and particularly in its clear-thinking chairman, Derek Davison, Iain Sproat saw the catalyst for change. There were two particular causes that were close to Davison's competitive heart.

One was bitterness over the charges the CAA were making for accepting aircraft on to the UK register. These had not been so significant to a monolithic State airline like British Airways, but they were a distinct burden to a smaller independent. Behind the scenes, Davison and his team put much homework into their pleas for a price reduction. This included the production of a compelling dossier which even won the admiration of civil servants who, over the years, had been caught in the slipstream of what they considered ill-conceived, ill-judged and ill-prepared submissions from some other airline chiefs.

The second contentious issue was the equally high charges which were being levied for airline meteorological reports. The softening of attitudes on both these matters owes much to Britannia's persuasive input.

That is not to say there was personal, or even professional, animosity between Britannia and bodies like the Civil Aviation Authority. Sir Nigel Foulkes, in his days as chairman of the CAA from 1977 to 1982, maintains that Britannia was the best run of the British airlines, and his successor, Sir John Dent, readily attests: "We never had a problem with Britannia. Everything was absolutely first class from an operational and safety aspect – and it was not every company you could say that about."

It turned out that such efficiency and effectiveness created its own problem. Some of the regulations which had to be imposed by the CAA were to meet the potentials for disaster that could be created by any operator who might have less than perfect standards. As a result, the up-to-scratch airlines, like Britannia, had to suffer what might appear to them unnecessary red-tape.

"Unfortunately," says Sir John, "the whole of the industry is not like Britannia, and I think Derek Davison sometimes saw our regulations as interference. They were, of course, aimed at maintaining the standards of the industry and not the standards of Britannia. I think he failed to understand how near to the edge some of the operators were, and how much regulation was required to keep up the high standards that the UK achieved. He believed we over-regulated."

Sir John Dent instances the question of the high price and the procedures for placing aircraft on the UK register, particularly in the way it affected the Boeing 737s.

"If we were dealing with Britannia only then it could have been different, but we had so many airlines all operating these aircraft that we had to impose the standards that we believed necessary. The result is that the efficient suffer for the inefficient, but then the honest man always suffers because of the criminal."

A contentious arena which Britannia entered gladiatorially was the politically-charged fight surrounding the privatisation of the State-owned British Airways. It began in 1984, with regular skirmishes throughout a protracted campaign which eventually ended in BA's flotation in 1987.

The independents had differing priorities within that scenario. The most vociferous in his views, at least in public, was Sir Adam Thomson, chairman of British Caledonian, who felt that a substantial re-allocation of routes should accompany BA's privatisation. He issued 'blue books' and 'gold books' outlining his airline's case. He felt that his was the 'second force' able to compete comprehensively on scheduled routes with British Airways and he was fighting for a 23 per cent reduction of BA's scheduled services which should be transferred to B.Cal and other independents.

The anxiety of Britannia, however, was that a private enterprise British Airways would unfairly be able to flex its huge muscles in the de-regulated charter market supported by profits on protected scheduled routes. It was not avaricious for any BA scheduled routes.

Britannia's proposal was that BA should be denied access to the whole 'plane charter market, with its charter subsidiary British Airtours either being absorbed into BA, or disposed of. This would be in exchange for the continuing protection of the State airline's scheduled routes.

Sir John Dent and his Civil Aviation Authority were well aware of the dangers. They saw a privatised British Airways emerging so strong that it could have a destructive effect on the rest of the industry. One of their solutions, on scheduled routes, was for the independents to build up strong 'hub' operations from provincial airports. It also recommended that the Authority be given stronger powers to control British Airways' activities in the charter market.

Many of the CAA's proposals were rejected when the Government published its White Paper 'Airline Competition Policy' in the autumn of 1984. It was a blow to Britannia, and this is how director, customer services and external affairs, Bob Parker-Eaton explained it in the airline's staff newspaper:

"The Government had the opportunity of using the occasion of privatisation to restructure British civil aviation to provide a balanced industry better able to face a free market future.

"Because the dominant giant will continue to exist virtually unchanged and with most of its unassailable advantages, market forces cannot be given free rein. The Government has recognised this, and the White Paper proposes careful monitoring by the CAA to prevent unfair practices and predatory pricing. Further new safeguards are proposed with the involvement of the Director General of Fair Trading and the Monopolies and Mergers Commission. In theory, the Government has sought to provide the necessary safeguards, although much remains to be done in defining the responsibilities and before we can be sure that the safeguards do indeed provide the necessary protection.

"Britannia's reaction to the White Paper is split into two areas: disappointment that the Government has failed to take the opportunity to restructure British aviation. This is an opportunity which may not recur for many years. The second reaction, which related to the likely direct impact of the privatised BA on Britannia, is of relief that the Government has apparently recognised the charter airline argument and has responded by proposing safeguards. Britannia sought no part of BA or its routes, thus this somewhat muted reaction is in contrast to that of some independent airlines which had sought advances and advantages for themselves.

"Much work remains to be done in translating the intentions of the White Paper into reality, and Britannia will continue to be active. Clearly the future will be different from the past, and the new circumstances will provide opportunities as well as threats. Britannia will tackle the future with its traditional flexibility."

The simmering discontent boiled up the following year when Britannia again submitted evidence to the Civil Aviation Authority applying, as they said, "to set a quantitative limit to British Airways' penetration of the UK originating leisure market".

In it they spoke strongly of the belief that if BA's incursion into the UK holiday market was not curbed, and seen to be curbed, they and most of the independent airlines would suffer inroads into their business "which will render it such as no longer to justify the investor confidence needed for their further development or survival in their present form".

They pointed out that the famous Edwards Committee report in 1969 into the future of UK civil aviation supported the development of a competitive multi-airline industry as the best way to meet consumer needs. But Britannia maintained that the benefits which BA got of high fares, protected market shares, capacity, pooled revenue with other airlines, and royalty agreements were now being used to compete with the UK independents.

"Where Britannia makes a complaint is that BA should not use the argument that it has to be 'strong' to compete with foreign airlines if it is then to use the products of that strength to damage the UK airline industry, and to destroy the effective competition which has existed within the UK-originating leisure market."

Britannia had maintained in an earlier submission that the British charter airlines' consistent profitability was against a background of a balanced competitive market. Unbalanced competition, they now said, "would clearly destroy this consistent profitability.

"Britannia continues to contend that, if it were BA's intention to put the charter airlines out of business, it would not be a costly exercise for it to do so. It is even less so today. Their overheads are down. Their aircraft written down. They may as well fly the routes as not."

The application concludes:

"The tide in the industry, particularly in the leisure side, which began to flow at the beginning of 1983, is now threatening the industry as never before in those areas where there is freedom of access, through liberal licensing policies, for British Airways and British Airtours to penetrate without difficulty into international charter/leisure markets previously developed by and shared among a group of financially healthy airlines, with relatively limited involvement of the State airline group. It is this freedom of access, linked to the available opportunities arising out of the many scheduled service licences already held by British Airways, which together present such a dangerous threat to the overall wellbeing of the industry."

It was, in the opinion of many observers, a telling case but, unfortunately for Britannia, the Civil Aviation Authority turned down the application on the grounds that "what has been demonstrated is that the European leisure sector of the industry remains competitive. British Airways is in a position to engage in anti-competitive behaviour . . . but there was no evidence that it has done so, is doing so, or is about to do so."

Britannia was not happy with that verdict and lodged an appeal which declared that "all involved in the industry accept that British Airways and British Airtours by reason of increased efficiency, changed aircraft, a Heathrow base and subsidy from other operations, are in a position to dump or place capacity in the whole plane charter market in volume, at will. This market is the only one in which the charter airlines, hitherto the most profitable and robust part of the industry, can operate – scheduled routes and foreign designations are not available to them. If this goes, investment will dry up and, with it, competition will cease, or at best be severely curtailed."

The undisputed leader of the charter airlines was trying to persuade the CAA to remedy the imbalance. Though they acknowledged that it existed, the Authority claimed not to have the power to act.

Despite this further plea, Secretary of State for Transport, John Moore, dismissed the appeal in the autumn of 1986 and refused to revoke any BA or Airtours licences. Though claiming that there was no evidence that British Airways had engaged in anti-competitive behaviour, he did concede that the case had demonstrated that "effective safeguards against anti-competitive behaviour and predatory pricing were essential to the success of the Government's airline competition policy". In view of this, he agreed that the CAA should review the information available to it on airlines' activities and consider whether it could be improved.

There was a feeling at their Luton headquarters that, although they had lost the battle, Britannia had won the long-running war. They were delighted that new safeguards would now be imposed and that the CAA had the authority to judge any contentious competitive situations that could arise in the future.

It was, coincidentally, about the same time that Britannia chairman Derek Davison was reminding readers of Airline Business magazine that the profitability of airlines in Europe measured in terms of return on capital – "which in the end will be the determining factor as more and more airlines become privatised" – was way below the returns available for funds invested in other sectors.

It was a comment which could equally serve to remind politicians of the fine balance between success and disaster in the volatile airline business.

Former chairman of the Civil Aviation Authority Sir John Dent who praises Britannia's operational standards.

CHAPTER FOURTEEN

Keeping them flying

Beginning with operations, the next five chapters take a look at various aspects of Britannia Airways' activities today.

Those who remember pictures of WAAFs in World War Two chalking the progress of the Battle of Britain on to blackboards at Fighter Command headquarters would, perhaps, experience déjà vu should they penetrate Britannia's operations room just within the entrance to Luton Airport.

The battle here, however, is not waged in shooting down the enemy but in shooting up the percentage of on-time departures. This, surprisingly at first impression, is undertaken by writing on wall charts to update the latest movement of all the aircraft in the airline's fleet. It might be felt that the only concession to progress is that the white chalk on blackboards for Spitfires and Hurricanes has given way, for Boeing 737s and 767s, to coloured felt pens on white melamine.

Each of these fleet aircraft has its own dedicated board so that, clustered in a semi-circular mural round the operations desk, are annotated movement charts for that day's flights, together with spares for aircraft of other airlines that might be chartered in to meet peak demands. Below them are the movement boards for the following day and, in the wings, like sentries waiting for the changing of the guard, are the skeletal schedules for succeeding days.

As duty staff climb the dais to update movements of Charlie Tango or Yankee Kilo, the obvious question to put to operations manager Martin Stirling is why all this is not computerised. The answer is simple. With a sweep of his eyes across the boards, the duty controller can immediately assess the state of the 175 sector flights that constitute a summer's day of operations. Substituting the embrace of the iris with a visual display unit would entail punching the keyboard many times to achieve the same breadth of knowledge.

That is not to say that modern technology does not play its part. Captains of the fleet are continually calling up the operations room with updates on their progress or to report snags with their equipment – those within a 200 miles radius use very high frequency bands and those penetrating remoter Europe or beyond turn to single side band high frequency radio. By the side of the controller is a computer terminal and, for instance, should a captain wish to divert to a non-scheduled airport for any reason, the availability of handling equipment and refuelling capability can immediately be keyed on to the screen. And behind the controller is a printer which punches out a variety of information including actual flight movement times for each individual aircraft.

The greatest asset a controller can possess, apart from calmness and judgment under stress, is the ability to act quickly to meet a sudden crisis.

Take what could be one of the worst, though unusual, situations. A Boeing 767 arrives in Tenerife just before midnight (all times in operations control are based on Greenwich Mean Time) with an unserviceable engine. It is due to load 270 passengers and take off in the early hours of the following day for Gatwick. If a replacement engine is needed, the passengers cannot be delayed awaiting the servicing of that aircraft as a new engine would have to be sent out in a freighter together with engineers to fit it.

So the duty controller would have to notify the engineering department of the problem, arrange to charter a freighter, secure a substitute aircraft to fly the stranded passengers home, and then, should the rest of the Britannia fleet be fully occupied, hope to secure the charter of an aircraft at short notice to carry out the succeeding day's programme of the out-of-action Boeing 767.

There is also the knock-on effect for the crew rostering department which has an office adjoining the operations room. At any one time, even without sudden crises, they are scheduling crews for up to 1,400 different flights.

It is acknowledged by everyone within the company that the quality of their rostering affects morale to a greater degree than any other single discipline in the airline. A specific roster is completed at least four weeks ahead of the flight. The crews can, therefore, arrange their social and domestic life around it. Equally, judicious organising of staff can have a significant effect on airline costs from the planning stage to the sort of hypothetical crisis typified by the Boeing 767 in Tenerife. The way they meet the problems, from arranging crew hotel accommodation right down to transport to get them there, can be financially critical.

One aspect of the layout of the operations centre at Luton today still owes its origins to the earliest days of Euravia. In that first wooden building which served as the complete administrative facility, the only way non-operations staff could gain access to the operations team was through a small hatch. Today none of the pilots or crew is allowed into the much bigger operations centre. The reasoning for this is that the controllers are responsible for the whole of the Britannia flying schedule including Gatwick, Manchester and the other UK departure points. Therefore, just because a crew is flying from Luton, it is illogical that they should have direct access whereas those based at other airports cannot.

▲

Above *Britannia's operations room at Luton Airport showing the boards which display the progress of up to 175 sector flights a day.*

Below *The visual display unit in the ops. room on which aircraft arrival and departure signals are received from UK and overseas stations.*

The operations division's forward planning department as it looked in 1974 before computerisation. Checking the boards (left to right) *are Dave Hills, operations planning officer, Trevor Caveney, operations supervisor, and Dave Cox, operations manager, in the posts they held at that time.*

Originally, the operations room was a separate entity from crew planning which resulted in the controller shifting aircraft round and, in effect, claiming that if crew could not be found to meet the change then it was not his fault.

It was Roy McDougall, when he was operations director, who made them one department with 24 hours crewing. Many of the staff are now dual qualified on operations and crew rostering. Changes are no longer made to aircraft schedules unless crews can be found to operate them.

This system was introduced following a French air traffic controllers work-to-rule industrial action which emphasised the weakness of not having a co-ordinated set up. Even then, the master stroke of sending a Britannia executive to France to liaise with their air traffic control worked wonders for continuing co-operation.

The masterminding of all this activity is now under operations director Stu Grieve. His predecessor in the post, Dave Hopkins, regards that 1978 French strike and its consequent delays as a watershed.

"Controlling and operating through that period did accelerate a new look at the way operations were organised. I believe that what we have today is a result of that watershed – the day-to-day crewing on one side and the operation of the aeroplane on the other, and a supervisor effectively over the whole operation. I think the operations department today does a far better job. It is more experienced, makes the right decisions the vast majority of the time, and has really strengthened itself considerably over the years."

The main change in those intervening years is the reliance that is now placed on computers to store the total operational programme. Having a complete system also helps avoid mistakes. Rosters for crews come out of computers, whereas before typists took two or three days to type them from original master rosters. And, invariably, mistakes were made.

Another computer-aid to efficiency and time-saving is that Britannia's operations supervisors now have a direct input into United Kingdom air traffic control for aircraft flight 'slot' times. Previously they had to telephone the centre, near Heathrow Airport, and ask for a slot. This could take up to an hour to obtain. Now the request is carried instantly over a computer network.

▲ *Operations director Stu Grieve masterminds all the operations activities, the nerve centre of which is located in the airline's Luton headquarters.*

The hectic summer season of 1986 would have been extremely difficult to operate successfully without computers. Utilisation of aircraft was 25 per cent up on the previous year, with a near parallel increase in crew utilisation.

This was reflected on those wallboards round the operations room. Each of them accounted for 14 flights a week in 1985, but this was boosted to 18 flights in 1986. Aircraft were undertaking up to 105 hours of flying a week compared with the previous 80 hours.

Few in the corridors or hangars at Luton would be willing to bet that those figures can be beaten in future years. When maintenance and other needs are taken into account, those impressive hours are regarded as close to the maximum utilisation for these aircraft based on Britannia's present operation.

CHAPTER FIFTEEN

Men of power

The range of tools and instruments an aircraft engineer needs is as varied as those of a surgeon in an operating theatre. This kit is used for engine maintenance.

For a Britannia Airways' Boeing 737 to be flying 105 hours a week is the equivalent of being constantly airborne for more than four days out of the seven. Though far from a direct comparison, a scheduled carrier, British Airways, in its year to March, 1986, averaged 50 hours a week on its 737 fleet – or just over two days' flying.

Not surprisingly, therefore, chairman Derek Davison asserts that "Britannia is very proud of its engineering division – and with every justification!" For the challenge of keeping aircraft flying with that intensity of workload is formidable.

Its 750 engineering staff, its two large hangars, its numerous specialist workshops all combine to support enormously high levels of activity during the summer months and those utilisations which have consistently been the highest in the world for the 737 and the highest for the Boeing 767 engaged in the comparative short ranges of Britannia's operation.

Preventative maintenance is the key to the engineering contribution to that high work rate. A standard of excellence is required in all activities, from the stripping-down of the aircraft to mere shells in order to examine and repair the structure during the winter to the engine and component overhaul monitored by Britannia, whether in-house or contracted. Also, the responses required when, in spite of all the preventative activities, inevitable unserviceabilities occur.

In order to ensure excellent standards are maintained, Britannia's independent inspection force responsible to the chief inspector constantly monitors activity. The training for many tasks is lengthy and demanding and the skills of a very high order. Five or six years' training is not uncommon.

Britannia's engineering division today is the envy of many, with tooling, test equipment and skills covering aircraft maintenance, modification and overhaul approved by the Civil Aviation Authority of Britain and the Federal Aviation Administration of the United States. It attracts

Maintenance taking place (left) *on a Boeing 737 Pratt & Whitney JT8D engine and* (right) *a 767 General Electric CF6 engine.*

customers from all over the world seeking not the cheapest but high standards of cost-effective maintenance. This was not always so.

Luton was not the easiest place to attract the skills required for such an organisation. Success breeds success and as Britannia grew in status and ability to offer attractive careers to engineers, it became progressively easier to recruit.

Jimmy Little, Britannia's first technical director, was instrumental in bringing about the change from a keen but struggling organisation, when he joined in 1965, to a very professional organisation when he retired in 1980.

Geoff Parkins and Bill Buxton later made their significant contributions, but today it is in the hands of Bernard Newton who proudly admits: "Right from the canteen staff to the management, what never ceases to amaze me is the obvious enthusiasm of the staff. You just cannot get high utilisation unless your team is organised and dedicated."

This dedication proved itself over the winter of 1986–87 when Britannia's most ambitious ever engineering maintenance programme resulted in a workload of 154,000 manhours following the record 107,000 flying hours during 1986.

That certainly did not allow any time for third-party activity apart from continuing work on the VC-10 fleet for the Ministry of Defence. But Bernard Newton and his men are now determined to build on their outside aircraft maintenance activities which have already covered Europe, the United States, Canada, Africa and the Middle East. It is Africa which, perhaps, offers the greatest future potential. In 1986, the overseas earnings for maintenance and aircrew training contracts amounted to more than £3 million, but there is great confidence that this can be significantly increased in the years ahead.

Seeing the possibility of outside contract work – particularly at periods when their own in-house activity is not at its most intense – Britannia is geared up to offer maintenance on different types of aircraft, the Boeing 727 being a prime example. Work has been carried out for airlines varying from Air Europe to Air Tanzania, but one of their quick-action responses, which gave much pride, was for the big carrier, American Airlines. During the summer of 1986, one of their Boeing 767s developed undercarriage

An important contract for Britannia's engineering department has involved the VC-10 fleet of the Royal Air Force.

problems on a flight from Munich to Chicago via Dusseldorf. The passengers were off-loaded at Dusseldorf and the aircraft flown to Luton. It landed at 2100 hours and was towed into Britannia's £4 million special 767 hangar. Having jacked up the airliner, engineers discovered that a downlock actuator on the main undercarriage was malfunctioning. A replacement was fitted and the aircraft was serviceable 4½ hours later.

The advent of the Boeing 767 hangar provided for the further development of the airline's ability to offer comprehensive aircraft and component maintenance services to other airlines, domestic and foreign.

The Britannia engineering base, which today is spread imposingly on both sides of Luton International Airport's parking ramp, has been traditionally self-reliant in developing its range of equipment. The airline's engineers have used their ingenuity to produce a lot of their own equipment rather than buying-in expensive items. It is a successful policy which continues.

There are a number of component workshops. The electrical shop tests, maintains and repairs a wide variety of equipment, from landing lights, cooling fans, water heaters and actuators to galley ovens and toilet pumps. This capability has been developed in-house. Once the decision was taken by Britannia to repair its own electrical components, the workshops supervisor and staff equipped the facility from scratch. He and his enthusiastic colleagues have devised and assembled most of the equipment themselves and brought it on-line.

"They are looking to increase their capability all the time," Bernard Newton reports. "For instance, when the 767 came into the fleet as a new aeroplane, as the components were taken off the aircraft they examined them and judged whether it was possible to carry out servicing on them in-house. Obviously there is a cost effectiveness study to evaluate how much it will cost to set up the test procedures and whether they can be repaired by us."

Newton emphasises that the aim is not a comprehensive facility like the Boeing company's own establishment in the UK, which has £½ million of computer testing equipment alone, but rather a support workshop.

"We are not on that scale, but nevertheless the engineering team have saved the company a lot of money. And there is no doubt about it, one of the beauties of having your own workshop is that you are in control of your own destiny as far as turnround times are concerned for components."

Another workshop example is the repair and test facility for avionics equipment. This embraces flight deck and cabin communications, a variety of air traffic control instruments, radar, the flight data recorder, and a host of other instruments. Because much of this equipment is advanced state-of-the-art, there is a greater need to buy highly sophisticated test apparatus from outside sources. The avionics workshop is the longest established of all the workshops.

Other facilities within the engineering complex at Luton include the power plant bay and departments for hydraulic, mechanical and pneumatic components, metal heat treatment, wheels and brakes, safety equipment and oxygen, aircraft weighing, a cutting, bending, forming and welding unit, and a paint shop.

More recently, they have been moving into the repairing and renewal of fibreglass and composite components employed in the latest technology aircraft. The techniques for this work are very complex.

The setting up and staffing of a maintenance and support unit for Britannia's simulators is a comparatively new challenge for the airline starting with the acquisition of the 737 followed by a 767 stemming from the agreement between Braathens of Norway and Britannia jointly to purchase a 767 simulator.This was based at Luton because of its relatively superior access to potential world users compared with Oslo.

Above *A Boeing 737 undergoing a major check at Luton.*

Left *Work for other airlines is a growing activity for Britannia's engineers. This distinctive logo belongs to an Air Tanzania 737.*

Britannia
BOEING 767

◄

This £4 million hangar, Parkins House, was built at Luton by Britannia to house their wide-bodied 767s, and named after their late technical director, Geoff Parkins. Above, the then Aviation Minister, David Mitchell, unveils the commemorative plaque at the opening of the hangar, watched by Mrs Elizabeth Parkins and Britannia chairman Derek Davison.

Above *One of 1,500 wheels which are inspected and overhauled each year.*

Above right *The interior of a Boeing 737 during a major inspection.*

While the objective in designing a simulator is to make it operate in motion – visually and in handling characteristics – as close as possible to the aeroplane, that does not hold true for maintenance. Maintenance and support of simulators is just about as different from maintenance of aeroplanes as it could be, with near total involvement in avionics. Certainly the hydraulic jacks which provide the movement require maintenance from time to time, but the real investment and challenge to the maintenance team lies in the huge banks of computer equipment, the software required and the interface with the visual, movement and tactile simulation.

In all this work, developments in engineering technology give today's engineers great advantages. One is the ability to make a judgment on whether an engine needs to be taken out of service without having to strip it down, thanks to boroscopic equipment and photography using fibre optics. The big assets of this are explained by Newton:

"The consequences of leaving an engine in service when it really should be attended to can be far more expensive and serious. In the old days of the Constellation's Cyclone engines, you had little warning of impending trouble. They would just stop and perhaps the cylinder head could detach. But now we have tools which give us far greater ability to make sound judgments. Of course, our experience and that of the manufacturers contribute a great deal to making that judgment."

The other advantage of today is in the construction of the engines themselves. The big difference between the JT8-D of the 737 and the CF6 of the 767 is that, as the wide-bodied aircraft engine is completely modular, there is no need to strip the majority of the engine for a specific and possibly minor malfunction. The exhaust module or the turbine section, for instance, can be removed in isolation and either repaired or replaced with another module.

Constant review of engine performance in service has a substantial pay-back potential. Even small adjustments to an engine can be significant in terms of performance. These could result in a fuel saving and, as Bernard Newton says realistically: "We buy aeroplanes to help run a business and make some money. Safety, of course, always was and always will be supremely important, but aircraft performance is so vital now we must get every aspect right in order to gain the best returns for the business."

There is, however, another major engineering sunrise on the horizon which would greatly enhance the Britannia engineers' ability to spot potential trouble well in advance. They are moving towards the automatic monitoring on the ground of the performance of engines while the aircraft themselves are still in the air flying to or from their holiday destinations.

When Bernard Newton surveys the sophisticated equipment he has today for dealing with technical problems, he might well think back to the flight twenty or so years ago when he was a 'flying spanner' on a Bristol Britannia. His job was to deal with any snag that might occur on ground stops during a charter from Hong Kong to the UK bringing back a ship's crew.

When they reached Dubai, there was no ignition on the Britannia's number four engine. The only course seemed to be to unload the sailors and ferry the aircraft back to Britain. The young, enthusiastic Newton had other ideas. He opened the cowling and removed the ignitor plug from the engine, and then had a thought. All he told the flight deck crew was that, when he gave the thumbs-up sign, they were to press the starter button.

Meanwhile he found a piece of rope a few inches long and soaked it in fuel. Young Bernard put one end in the ignitor plug hole, then lit the other with a match. When the cord was burning with a good flame he pushed it further in with his finger and quickly put the plug back. He gave the thumbs up sign to the flight deck, they hit the button, and the result was a perfect light-up. There was just one more trick to perform – closing the cowling which was only about nine inches behind the 16-foot long whirling propeller blades.

They were on their way again – but there was one final hiccup. The engine would not re-ignite on the last staging stop in Athens. So the intrepid 'flying spanner' had to carry out the same ingenious solution all over again.

"It is not like that anymore," he says today, perhaps a little wistfully.

▲ *Technical director Bernard Newton who in the early days sometimes acted as a 'flying spanner'.*

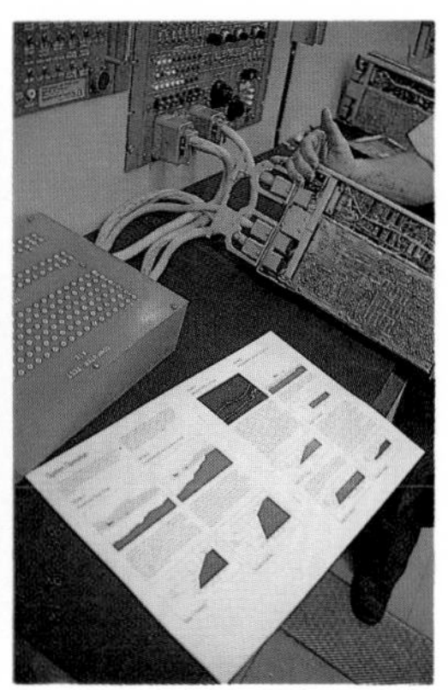

◄ *Testing of* (far left) *an aircraft weather radar system and* (immediate left) *a ground proximity warning system.*

CHAPTER SIXTEEN

Looking after the customers

➤

Opposite *Britannia is justifiably proud of its cabin staff, a vital link in projecting the company's image to its passengers.*

At the end of 1973, Wing Commander Robert Parker-Eaton was listening (perhaps not too intently) to a lecture on the planning of urban motorways on a post-graduate transport course at Leeds University. He was pulled from the lecture to take a telephone call from the then managing director of Britannia Airways, John Sauvage. The call contained an unexpected invitation for Parker-Eaton to resign his commission and join Britannia to head the customer services division. Parker-Eaton, an RAF transport specialist awarded the MBE for his work with both military and civil transport, did not require much time for thought, despite expectations of a good career ahead of him. He accepted the challenge and joined Britannia's team.

Bob Parker-Eaton had got to know Britannia, and vice versa, some years earlier, when the airline first won the Ministry of Defence contract to fly troops and their families to and from Germany. He was then in charge of all civil air trooping and had helped Britannia to 'work-up' the new contract. Of all the British airlines, Britannia had most impressed him. "Only Britannia could have persuaded me from the RAF," he says.

"For my brief I was told to pull together every activity where the passenger came into contact with the airline – cabin staff, their recruitment, training and management, the traffic department, airfield handling contracts, catering, duty free sales and in-flight services." Later, when Parker-Eaton joined the board at the beginning of the Davison era, public relations and security were added to these responsibilities.

Although the various departments performed to high standards, the management structure and organisation were those of a very small, young company, and not capable of coping with likely expansions and the pressures which would accompany that growth.

On the 'support' side, the department reflected the prime needs of the early years – to keep the airline flying. The jacks-of-all-trades were

➤

Customer services and external affairs director Bob Parker-Eaton says Britannia was the only airline that could have persuaded him to leave a promising career in the RAF.

expert on quick turnrounds, loading aircraft and of achieving their ends by personal contact and example. Practical people, essential in those early days, they were less interested in the bureaucratic chores of letter writing, buying, budgeting and delegating. Duty free sales were seen to be important; product selection, purchase and promotion were not. As one manager at the time expressed it: "A monkey could do that job." Tight control of costs, practised within the operation, did not extend to purchasing. And yet the size of the airline was already such that even pennies saved on a single item could produce huge benefits.

For two years, Parker-Eaton personally responded to every passenger letter of complaint or appreciation. Complaints, fortunately, were few, because of the high standards and personal commitment of that original loyal staff. But they were already at full stretch. The aftermath of the oil crisis, increasing competition, and company growth would require a totally different approach.

Britannia operated through so many airfields and required so many varied services which it could not possibly satisfy itself. This called into question the 'jack-of-all-trades' approach. What the airline needed were managers who were specialist, tough buyers, who could establish the required standards, and then maintain those standards by quality control checks and by motivating the suppliers, and be innovative.

A new breed of manager grew within the 'support' side of customer services. Some were promoted from within. Others, mainly specialists, were recruited.

The new professionals in the organisation which was established

The cabin crew uniform of the early seventies, in the era of mini skirts.

soon had to face the challenges of rapid growth, planning for and introducing the Boeing 767, and of staying ahead of increasingly efficient competitors. The way in which the traffic department set about achieving the essential 45 minute turnrounds of the 767s overseas – and their success – has already been described.

Britannia's innovations in in-flight services – such as the introduction of video and audio entertainment and the display units in the cabin on all aircraft giving readouts on height and speed throughout the journey – have benefitted the passenger and given the airline an edge over its competitors. And developments are in train to provide even more in-flight information to interest the passenger.

As mentioned, Britannia sells more goods in-flight than any other airline in the world. That selling prices are competitive, and margins good, owes much to the buying and marketing skills of Jack Moss and his in-flight services team.

Flight catering manager Jenny Groom, a highly qualified catering and food specialist, has to select menus and contract the supply of meals from around forty airfields scattered across Europe. "My most difficult task," she says, "has been to ensure that Mediterranean flight kitchens provide a genuine good British hot breakfast, perhaps our passengers' favourite meal." Her constant visits, involving much sampling of such basic items as baked beans and sausages, must have worked. Passengers are invariably surprised to learn that the very British breakfast for which many have been yearning since they left for their holiday, and which they enjoyed on their homebound flight, was prepared in Spanish or Greek kitchens.

A striking contrast with the picture on the opposite page. Both the present summer and winter uniforms are practical as well as elegant.

In 1985, Bob Parker-Eaton delegated the responsibility for running all the 'support' departments to Gerry Bryant, who was promoted to the post of general manager, passenger services. Bryant's task is to maintain Britannia's leadership over its competitors, as always, cost effectively.

When Bob Parker-Eaton arrived at Britannia, the challenge of cabin services was different from that of the 'support' departments, but again was made easier by the existing high standards and motivation of the cabin staff.

Management consisted of a chief stewardess, Jacky Clayton, and a tiny team. They knew each stewardess by her first name – they had recruited every single one by personal interview. They could maintain leave rosters, ensure smartness and would monitor standards by checking flights. In the original, small, airline these efforts produced results, for in a small airline personal motivation and identification are relatively easy to achieve. Because so much management time was taken in recruitment, the department operated for several months a year effectively without leadership.

Serving drinks on a Boeing 767. Self-motivation of cabin staff is essential.

Much later, that self-motivation of cabin staff became the key to the management system which was adopted. At the time, though, it was obvious that changes were urgently needed if the airline continued to grow, without the deterioration in cabin staff attitudes so obvious in many larger airlines. The hope was that managers could be developed within the department, rather than introducing professional, non-cabin staff managers from outside as did most larger airlines.

Formal management training was not successful. The jargon and the content was daunting and appeared to the participants not to relate to their own situations. Nor did the courses help in revealing management potential in the group of service-minded cabin staff.

Jacky Clayton and Bob Parker-Eaton visited airlines around the world to see how they tackled the problem. Not one was pleased with its set-up. As Bob Parker-Eaton recalls: "More often than not, we were met with the comment that they were hoping to learn from us!" There appeared to be a point in the growth of an airline when management lost effective control and staff attitudes deteriorated. Clearly, Britannia had not reached that point, but could well do so. If other airlines could not help, perhaps a new approach was needed. But what? How could the undoubted qualities of the small airline be applied to one much bigger?

The breakthrough occurred when Parker-Eaton read a paper written by an American aviation consultant, Charles Butler. Butler had been involved with the cabin services departments of TWA and Frontier Airlines. He had evolved a theory of applying a form of management by objectives to cabin services. MBO was no new theory – indeed, by then, it had been overtaken by newer management dogma. What was new was its application to a service industry in which management is absent at the workplace – the aircraft cabin.

The concept, heavily modified to make it acceptable for Britannia, began from the start point that cabin staff were good performers. For their performance to be maintained or improved, then even better self-motivation was necessary. This could be best achieved by improved two-way communication, seeking to remove or reduce the myriad of job irritants, more involvement in matters affecting the staff, by recognising performance, and by encouragement.

A new level of junior managers, called co-ordinators, was created. MBO, perhaps here better called Management by Commitment, helped to channel, and to measure, the performance of co-ordinators. Now they could see, and take pride in, quantifiable results. The allocation to them of specific cabin staff, in whom they were expected to take a genuine interest, helped to maintain the small airline identity and loyalties.

Britannia was, and is, genuinely proud of its cabin staff and cared for

▲ *Passengers absorbed in the audio and video entertainment which is a feature of Boeing 767 flights.*

them. It wished to keep them informed, honestly, of what was happening. It needed their views. The co-ordinator was the medium for all this, and, as a part of the measurement of co-ordinator performance, the opinions of the cabin staff are sought, by questionnaire, on many different aspects. Their answers, given mathematical values, help to measure the performance of their co-ordinators. So, too, do other items such as the in-flight sales of each allocated group. Perhaps the two most important attributes required of Britannia cabin staff are positive attitude and team work. Much effort is expended, right from the recruitment stage, to achieve this.

In the development of this new system, mistakes were made. Nevertheless, the care and concern for their cabin staff is the most noticeable feature of the regular management meetings.

Along with the original management system, recruitment, too, has been changed fundamentally. For 1986, the cabin services department received and processed some 15,000 applications. By careful vetting of the detailed application form, this number was whittled down to around 1,600 who were called for interview. Of these, 400 were offered contracts.

This huge task, repeated every year, is undertaken most successfully by the cabin services department, headed by Margaret Johnston who succeeded Jacky Clayton in 1985. Top managers are no longer involved. Rather, senior line cabin staff help to recruit their own peers. The session includes an interview as well as an elementary mathematics test. However, most store is placed on the group work – an aspect borrowed from the Services' commissioning methods. A group of applicants around a table are given topics and problems to discuss in a relaxed atmosphere. Here, they are closely watched. Attitude and team work – not brilliant individuality – are what is sought.

The 1986 demands on recruitment, training and operating – with almost 400 new recruits and close to a total of a thousand cabin staff – were the biggest to date in the history of Britannia, and the absorption of so many new, inexperienced staff over a very short period put the department to the test.

In 1986, Britannia received more letters of appreciation than in any other year. Passenger ratings of cabin staff and in-flight service equalled the highest ever and were ahead of all competitor airlines. Not surprisingly, Britannia was named Charter Airline of the Year by the British travel trade.

CHAPTER SEVENTEEN

Training hard

More than half a century ago, in the genteel era of flying boats, captains on the African routes would join their handful of passengers in the lounge of an hotel after an en route overnight stop. Over a cup of coffee, they would suggest that, if it was convenient to them, they might soon resume their journey. Would half an hour's time be suitable?

On trans-Atlantic flights, before retiring to their on-board beds, passengers would place their shoes on the cabin floor for a steward to polish during the night and return them before breakfast.

Two examples of what was included in flight deck and cabin crew training in those far-off leisurely, pioneering days. Neither coffee etiquette nor shoe-shining technique appears in today's training manuals of Britannia Airways. Though the comfort – and safety – of the passengers is still the paramount consideration, the jet era calls for in-flight training sophistication involving all the latest technological and managerial skills.

In their 25th birthday year, Britannia were employing a record of more than 400 flight-deck crew as well as those one thousand cabin staff. For both, the training not only embraces new entrants but also constant refresher and re-training courses and examinations for those on the payroll. There is, of course, one fundamental difference between the two disciplines. Pilots come to Britannia having already undergone intensive aviation schooling – in some cases followed by employment by other airlines or in the Forces – whereas, with few exceptions, stewardesses are trained from scratch.

Chief Pilot Chris Norman, who was previously chief training captain, followed one accepted career pattern. He was sponsored from school by Britannia as a cadet to the Oxford Air Training School and joined the airline in 1966. There followed a period with the then Skyways Coach Air company where he was sent by Britannia to gain experience of what it was like to be an airline pilot – undertaking eight flights a day certainly gained him that knowledge!

His first aircraft type on arriving at Luton was the turbo-prop Bristol Britannia. The only way then of converting to a new aeroplane was by actually flying the aircraft. It was the same a year later when he transferred to the newly-arrived Boeing 737. He was given twelve hours training on board the 737 which, even with pre-OPEC crisis fuel prices, involved appreciable expenditure.

The equipment which, in both cost and effectiveness terms, revolutionised aircrew training was the flight simulator.

A simulator authentically reproduces flying conditions by incorporating an exact replica of a flight deck. This not only moves on hydraulically operated legs as a result of the pilot's guiding the controls in the cockpit, but, whether the aircraft is programmed to be on the ground or in the air, a forward projector screen realistically reproduces the outside scene.

The first simulator bought by Britannia was for Boeing 737 training. It was purchased from CAE of Montreal, Canada, and in the eleven years it has been installed at Luton it has 'flown' well over 50,000 hours. In 1983, the airline took delivery of its £4½ million 767 simulator from Rediffusion Simulation in the UK. This included much later technology which is particularly reflected in the speed with which the computer works. The 767 model responds every 33 milliseconds so that the data can be looked at, and responded to, about a third quicker than for the 737. Consequently, for a pilot under tuition, this simulator feels much more like a real aeroplane, aided by wide-angled picture displays giving added

Above *The advent of the simulator has revolutionised flight deck training. This is the Boeing 767 simulator at Britannia's Luton base.*

Left *This multi exposure shot shows the gyrations of the simulator during a 'flight'.*

realism through a 150 degree uninterrupted field of view.

Today, a pilot converting to a Boeing 767 will spend 40 hours on the simulator. He is put through every conceivable problem which, however remotely, could occur on the aircraft in flight. It is training that could not be undertaken in the air because it would be unsafe to attempt some of the manoeuvres, and also because, particularly in today's climate, it would be prohibitively expensive to undergo 40 hours' actual flying. The crucial factor, however, is that simulator pilots are better trained because they can face a bigger variety of malfunctions and know how to deal with them correctly and promptly.

Even so, Captain Norman points out that they never put a pilot through events on the simulator which, in real life, would be unrealistic.

"There is no way we would simulate a wing falling off and ask the pilot what he intended doing about it. The aim is to show a pilot how he can do something about a problem he may possibly experience."

In crisis management, the most common ingredient of the training surrounds an engine failure or, more remotely, an engine fire or, even more remotely, a multi-engine failure. Britannia pilots are re-trained every half year on dealing with inoperative engines.

Some of the less daunting problems which figure in training are hydraulic failure, air conditioning and electrical malfunctions, and loss of pressurisation. On the Boeing 767, pressurisation is particularly important

Below *The Britannia 737 simulator.*

Below right *Famous racing driver Nikki Lauda, who runs his own airline, training in Britannia's 737 simulator.*

because there is need for prompt action when flying as high as 43,000 feet.

Not all problems on the flight deck, however, are technical in origin. There is the human factor, yet even here the simulator can play a vital role.

Norman explains: "The way a captain and first officer relate to each other on the flight deck is very important and very critical. This is especially so when the captain is more mature and we are introducing a young pilot to fly with him. With the age and experience gap, it is always possible for the senior man, if he is aggressive and overpowering, to shut the new pilot out of the operation. This has been a contributing factor in some accidents. That trait can be spotted in a simulator, providing an opportunity on debriefing the crew to eradicate the problem."

What is known as 'overloading' is another area for potential disaster.

"A pilot could instruct his junior, for example: 'Call the tower and tell them we are about to land. Put the gear down and read me the landing check while you're at it. I'll take flap forty.'

"The poor fellow receiving the instructions has his hands all over the place and, inevitably, one of the commands may not be complied with. We can observe tendencies like that on the simulator."

An important philosophical and practical approach Britannia adopt in their simulator training is what is called LOFT – line oriented flight

During a visit to Britannia Airways, Michael Brown (right), *president of the International Thomson Organisation, 'flew' the 767 simulator. With him is chief pilot Chris Norman, then flight training manager. Mr Brown successfully landed the 'aircraft' in Manchester at his first attempt.*

training. This was developed in the United States in the last decade, following the catastrophic Lockheed TriStar crash in the Florida Everglades. The accident was caused by the concentration of the flight deck crew on a faulty warning light in the cockpit to the exclusion of what was happening, in the meantime, to the flightpath of the aircraft. Captain Norman believes this disaster could have been avoided with the kind of flight deck management incorporated in LOFT simulator techniques.

"Quite simply, the simulator is treated as an aeroplane. That might sound very, very simple, but in a normal simulator training environment, as time is limited, an instructor tends to cover many malfunctions. Crew operating in a simulator can become quite stressful – that is why it is known as a 'sweat box' and, in many ways, the workload is quite unrealistic.

"What usually happens in a simulator is that the pilot is given instructions to operate round one home airport where he is given specific problems involving landings and take-offs. Incident reports have shown that this training is inadequate in today's world. Accidents tend to happen down route, a long way from home, and frequently they are not caused by one particular malfunction – not even by a malfunction at all, but by a breakdown in crew co-ordination.

"By training in real time – flying from one airport to another in real time all the way – you can study how crews work together. When we give them a malfunction, we see how they deal with it not around Luton or London Gatwick, but half-way across Spain or Germany. The weather may not be good, and they have to think what to do and where to go, including decisions on diverting to another airport. This real world situation is not normally undertaken on a simulator."

The real world ambiance is created right from the beginning, because, when the crew arrive at Luton for their simulator activity, Britannia staff issue them with all the normal paperwork involved in an actual flight – weather reports, navigation log, voyage report, technical log, and they also have a captain's briefing. They even work out what fuel they will need, and so they translate into an on-board-aircraft way of thinking.

Because Britannia Airways is essentially a charter airline, there are specific differences in other aspects of training. For instance, pilots with major scheduled carriers normally have a limited number of airports to which they fly, whereas Britannia pilots can be asked to fly to any of 70 or 80 different airports in Europe and Africa.

This is very demanding, and is one of the reasons accounting for a lower than normal pass rate on command courses for Britannia captains. A pilot entering command training with the airline will have a 60 per cent chance of passing his course, while on some other airlines it is as high as 90 or 95 per cent. This does not reflect on the standard of recruits wishing to move from the righthand to the lefthand seat on the flightdeck, but rather on the complexity and high standards sought for the operation.

What normally happens in conversion is that a first officer on a Boeing 767 is given a command on a 737 (only two pilots in the airline have dual designation on both aircraft, Captain Norman and operations director Stu Grieve). That in itself not only requires training in 'commandability', but also reconversion to the former type, which many of them may not have flown for some time.

The ratio in the fleet is about seven crews to each aircraft – 350 pilots for the 737s and 75 for the 767s. This entails a training team of 22 for the 737s and seven for the wide-bodied aircraft, and every six months each member of the crew is taken through re-training or testing by a member of the team. Additionally, there are yearly line checks when a member of the training team accompanies a pilot to a holiday destination on the flight deck. Training of new pilots, whether from school, the RAF or elsewhere, always takes place in the operationally slacker winter months.

A significant fact of the 1978–1979 period was the explosion in business which needed more than a hundred extra pilots. Managing director Dave Hopkins is sure that without the introduction of the flight simulator, training them would have been impossible. Those flight crew were, of course, for the Boeing 737s, but there was another similar training challenge for the 767 introduction, aggravated later when the heavy summer schedule of 1987 demanded that another 50 pilots be recruited.

When Hopkins became flight operations director in early 1982, a study was being made of how training of 767 crew was to be achieved, particularly in the light of the new technology involved in the aircraft.

"It would have been very easy to over-complicate the impact of the new aircraft, particularly as far as its electronic instruments were concerned. The case was put up, helped by Boeing and Braathens participation, that we should have our own simulator to be delivered before the first aircraft, unlike the 737 situation earlier. We were therefore able to undertake our own training on site, rather than at Boeing's facility, which would have been a very major disadvantage.

"Having bought a simulator, we saw its also being used as a cockpit procedures trainer. For the 737 we had a separate trainer for this purpose, but now we decided to have the 767 simulator and then degrade it for use as a cockpit procedures trainer. It was a positive step, because going out to buy a separate trainer would have been almost as costly as the simulator itself.

"From Day One, we were able to involve training using the hardware in the real role-type situation which enabled us to convert the pilots without any undue problems. It went extremely well – probably better than we expected. A lot of people worked very hard to make it come right – we must never be complacent in this business."

He believes that, despite pressure from outside Britannia, the decision to go for two-crew manning was a vital part of the 767 development.

Dave Hopkins maintains that a number of stepping stones taken in the evolution of the Boeing 737 in Britannia service were important in easing the potential trauma of conversion to the 767. One was the introduction of the Omega navigational aid as an alternative to the inertial system. One of its main advantages was the ability accurately to navigate round the Bay of Biscay to Spain, thus avoiding French air space. It enables a pilot to achieve greater route accuracy, particularly when flying to such destinations as the Canary Islands where there are less sophisticated external aids. It was calculated that Omega gained a saving of 36 seconds for each hour of flight. The important factor was that the pilots were getting used to using the number keyboard associated with Omega. A couple of years after that, the airline introduced a performance data computer system for the 737 which also incorporated a computer box with numbers to call up various parameters.

"Having already used these computer aids meant that the 767 technology was not such a big leap for our pilots as it might have been. It was, in fact, almost a non-event in that context, though, of course, a major event for the airline," Hopkins reports.

Just as flight deck crews have their simulators for training, so cabin crews have their own realistic mock-ups for 737 and 767 interiors, including fully-operational galleys and even smoke generators for emergency training. The training school also houses evacuation chutes.

Early recruits to the airline 25 years ago recall that the very first training lasted all of one week and took place in a cramped spare room in a wooden hut. The only aid to practical work then was a fire extinguisher.

It was still very much the same when the present cabin services training manager, Debbie Clifford, joined the airline in 1971. She was a young actress but, while 'resting', an ex-dancer girlfriend suggested she join Britannia for the six busy summer holiday months. After being told at her first interview to take her gloves off to make sure her hands were acceptable, and questioned on her father's job, there was a quick discussion after which she was asked when she could start. She had the week's training in the hut and then went straight on to three training flights.

Her memories were of having a bustling senior stewardess on her first flight, wonderful with the passengers but so full of energy that she virtually did all the work herself. The young Debbie thought she could never keep up that pace. Those were the months following the introduction of the Boeing 737 into service, and on a succeeding flight the senior stewardess said that in the 2 hours 20 minutes it would take to Alicante they could just serve the meal and give out duty free goods, but there would not be time to serve drinks. They had been used to the leisurely three hours or so that the old Britannia aircraft took to do the same journey.

Thanks to the sophisticated training of today, not only do passengers get their drinks on a 737, but with double the number of passengers carried on a Boeing 767 making the same journey, all 273 of them get drinks, a meal and their duty-frees.

Today, the Britannia training centre is in a new building with offices, five classrooms and the benefit of those aircraft mock-ups. The training itself matches these facilities in its professionalism.

New recruits are normally taken on in the spring for a short contract covering the busy summer months – at the end of that period the best of them might be offered a permanent career, subject to the operational needs at the time. Some of the summer intake could consist either of staff previously engaged by the airline or girls recruited from other airlines, but the majority would be young people between 19 and 27 raw to the

Stewardesses in the Boeing 767 galley mock-up during training at Luton.

▲ *Classroom work for cabin crew in the training school at Luton.*

airline industry.

Once they have been selected, they are passed to Debbie Clifford to place on training courses which last four weeks. Before that, they will have been handed a cabin staff information booklet which welcomes them and gives them potted background about the airline, the training, airline jargon, abbreviations and codes, the 24-hour clock, and foreign currencies. Personal guidelines vary from the wearing of earrings – 'only one in each ear, please!' – and a requirement that the length of hair-drop at the nape of the neck must be 'ten inches maximum and four inches minimum'. They are tested on the book on their first day. How much they have studied it is a good guide to their future enthusiasm and application.

The holiday business has been so buoyant in recent years – resulting in that record 400 new cabin staff for 1986 – that the original 9am to 5pm courses have given way to three shifts, one class being taught from 7am to 3.30pm, another 3.30pm to 11.30pm, and the third during a normal day.

The courses cover both safety training and cabin services. Safety is tackled first because it is recognised to be an intense subject, and should a pupil not be able to cope with that, then there would be little point in continuing to other aspects. Cabin services teaching includes practical classroom tuition such as fire-fighting, smoke training, and then passenger work, using the mock-ups, including serving drinks, meals, and duty frees, advice on special meals, meeting medical needs, as well as gaining rapport with passengers – and dealing with difficult ones.

Fellow pupils act as 'guinea pig' passengers in the cabin mock-ups, and Debbie Clifford admits they can be the worst passengers in the world. "Really rotten," she calls them.

What does she consider as the 'rottenest' real passenger? The one who has to pay for duty frees and then admits he doesn't have any sterling currency. "You tell him it will be perfectly all right to pay in Italian lira. After working out that it will be, say, 6250 lira he says he only has 4,450, and can he pay the rest in Spanish pesetas, which, again, you have to calculate. That can be a real problem when time is so limited."

The success of Britannia's cabin crew philosophy is based on attitude and teamwork. "That is what we try to get across in our courses," says Debbie Clifford. "This means, for instance, that in an emergency the crew know what is going to happen and feel confident about dealing with it and knowing what colleagues are also doing. It is intuitive."

She hopes that what was said to her by a passenger when she was herself a member of the cabin staff will be said to those she trains: "You really enjoy your job, don't you?"

It is to inculcate that spirit, as well as experience, that Britannia draw cabin crew members off line duty to become trainers themselves. And it is actual crew members who are the 'stars' of video training films which are now used extensively on courses. Several of these deal with the incidents which are considered most likely to occur on flights as a result of analysing reports regularly submitted by cabin staff. Debbie Clifford has vivid memories of the days when they used an American film. The trainees became convulsed with laughter when, in an emergency, a stewardess with a pronounced Brooklyn accent drawled "Grabe your ayncles" and another, when there was an attempted suicide on board, demurely murmured: "Please sir, don't worry about the mess. We'll clear it up!"

What is increasingly important in training, as has been proved by international hijack cases, is that there should be complete understanding between the flight deck and cabin crew. The Britannia courses now not only include emphasis on clarity and quickness of communication, but a line captain is introduced to the class so that they can cross-question him and gain a direct appreciation of what is required in a crisis.

Customer services director Bob Parker-Eaton re-emphasises the concepts developed in the previous chapter.

"A problem is that cabin staff are service people and they enjoy, or should enjoy, serving the public. So how do you make managers out of people who are non-management trained? We had to find a system to channel efforts along the lines we wanted them channelled." To do this, major resources were devoted to supervision and management development.

The bright men and women produced from this philosophy will form the backbone of the corporate body needed to take Britannia Airways into the last decade of the Twentieth Century.

Setting the sales

CHAPTER EIGHTEEN

When, in 1986, the results were published of an independent market research survey commissioned by Britannia Airways, the directors at Luton were not surprised by many of the findings. On the positive side, 97 per cent thought Britannia gave value for money, 84 per cent believed the airline had years of experience, 98 per cent accepted their good safety record, 79 per cent were aware they served good food, 88 per cent that they flew modern aircraft, and 91 per cent thought they treated passengers as individuals.

Despite all that, the negative picture was that only 31 per cent of those interviewed had a spontaneous awareness of the airline compared with 85 per cent for British Airways and 61 per cent for British Caledonian.

As the researchers diffidently pointed out: "Some aspects of image correction appear to be needed."

That is a fact not lost on Brian Christian, Britannia's commercial director. He had been planning controller for the airline and was one of the first promotions to the board made by Derek Davison after he became managing director. But as Christian saw it, the problem was not just the greater exposure to the public by scheduled airlines like BA and B.Cal through their advertising and sales promotion. In the seventies, he had already had to overcome a credibility gap within the travel trade itself.

"We had to recognise how tour operators perceived us. There was mistrust among many operators, because of our relationship with Thomson Holidays. The Thomson Group was seen as some sort of club, and operators felt they would be disadvantaged by dealing with an airline which had an in-house tour operator; they believed they would always come second in our priorities. We knew this was untrue, but we had to overcome this mistrust and set out to do so. We succeeded."

As a measure of this success, Brian Christian cites the fact that the proportion of the airline's business accounted for by Thomson Holidays moved from 75 per cent to 50 per cent.

"In bringing about this change, we have always pursued quality business that has long-term benefits for the airline. Short-term expediencies were never considered as a solution. And once other operators started flying with us, it did not take them long to be convinced that there was

The image of the airline has to be right, through from the tour operator to, as here, the smallest of passengers!

no disadvantage for them in our relationship with Thomson Holidays. All our customers are treated as equals. It couldn't work otherwise."

The other factor in this even-handedness is that Thomson Holidays do not use Britannia exclusively as their airline.

Britannia does not cater solely for the United Kingdom originating inclusive tour market – non-UK originating business now accounts for about ten per cent of Britannia's operations. Moves towards gaining this business began in the mid-seventies when there was some apprehension in the airline about having too high a proportion of revenue dependent on flying holidaymakers to Spanish resorts. It was not considered good corporate commonsense to be over-reliant on one dominant geographical sector when there were other reliable market segments.

A factor in this thinking, as Brian Christian explains, is that business originating overseas tends to have more stability than the UK inclusive tour market, which can fluctuate in one year by as much as 20 per cent. In addition, tour operators will sometimes be forced to make changes to their planned programmes in an effort to maintain their competitive edge, and go for a smaller volume programme giving a higher load factor and therefore a higher return, or give more concentration to a specific geographical area which offers particularly attractive prices. This is less likely to occur with the overseas originating business.

One appreciable element of Britannia's foreign traffic is from Italian families visiting their relatives in the UK, and Italians working there going home on holiday. This business alone amounts to a quarter of a million people a year. Another is the contract Britannia has held for a number of years to operate scheduled services on behalf of GB Airways between Gatwick and Gibraltar.

Britannia is also in a favourable position to increase its business in the inbound tourism market, and is doing so. The airline can achieve a much higher unit yield by bringing Scandinavians, French or Italians into the UK. Because wages are higher on the Continent, customers are willing to pay more for their tickets and, as a result, tour operators can pay more to the airlines. Where Britannia scores is that indigenous airlines in Europe also suffer from higher costs, and it is therefore difficult for them to compete for this business against British charter companies.

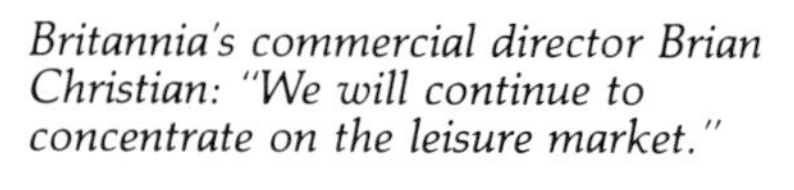

Britannia's commercial director Brian Christian: "We will continue to concentrate on the leisure market."

As far as the British leisure market is concerned, Brian Christian is convinced that it is nowhere near saturation point. Only 62 per cent of the 55 million population presently take a yearly holiday. And of those 34 million, just 9.5 million go on air package holidays. There is, therefore, still a lot of opportunity in the market, even allowing for those who refuse to fly and those who cannot afford to.

"However, airlines can never grow consistently in line with the market," explains Christian. "It has to be in fits and starts because of aircraft size. But we can start to take some of the opportunities on offer now."

One example is Britannia's entry into scheduled service operations. Their first scheduled service, from Manchester to Palma, began in May, 1985, almost 23 years to the day after that first Constellation flight left on the same journey. This 'first' was followed by other scheduled services from Manchester to Malaga in Spain, and Tenerife and Las Palmas in the Canary Isles. Tenerife and Las Palmas are also served with scheduled services from London Gatwick – and more are planned.

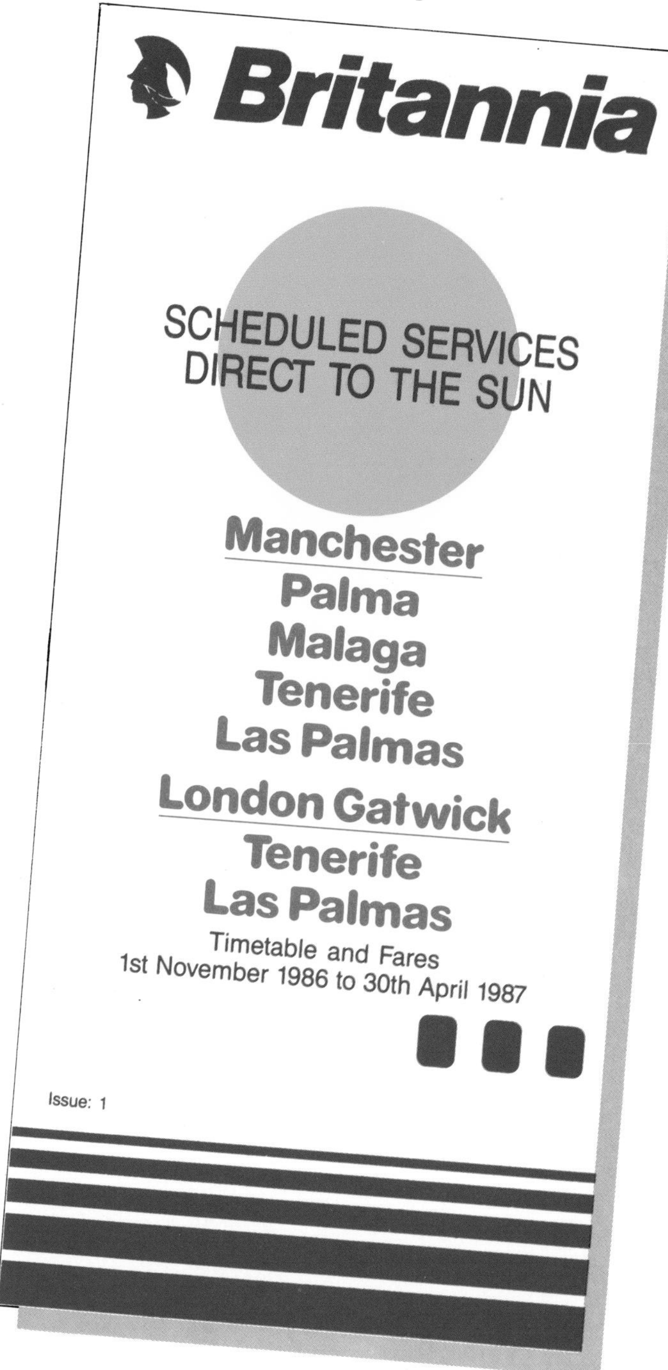

Britannia's scheduled services timetable, with flights to the sun from Manchester and London Gatwick.

The holiday starts here. Britannia's check-in desks at Luton International Airport.

One reason for the airline's introduction of scheduled services is the growing demand from holiday-makers who wish to make their travel and accommodation arrangements separately. But increasing pressure from foreign airlines, particularly in Spain, for a greater share of the charter business from the UK was also a factor in the decision to establish a scheduled presence on the most popular routes.

"We began the services on a minimal basis to avoid losses, but at the same time offering a proper scheduled operation," explains Brian Christian. But he emphasises that they are not, in any way, setting out to change the face of the airline's mainstream business. "The scheduled side will grow in the future, but charter will still be our major activity, and, where we do apply for new scheduled routes, they will continue to be those catering for the leisure market."

In 1986, for the first time ever, Britannia carried over five and a half million passengers, a considerable increase on its previous best year of 4.5 million which suggests little reason to change its philosophy.

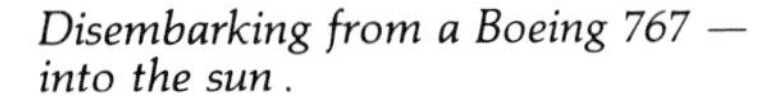

Disembarking from a Boeing 767 — into the sun.

Flightpath into the second quarter century

CHAPTER NINETEEN

Chairman and chief executive Derek Davison: praise for all his team.

As Britannia Airways confidently grips its boarding pass for the corporate flight into its second quarter century, chairman Derek Davison reflects on the first 25 years, looks to the challenges and opportunities ahead, and gives a fascinating insight into how he sees leisure aviation developing to the 21st century.

He looks back objectively on the era when the airline began. "With great excitement, great drive and great enthusiasm, a small number of people became involved in the creative, hard work necessary to get the airline on the road when there were some vital and significant decisions that had to be made. Firstly, they were taken by Ted Langton, then by Langton and Jed Williams, and later by Williams on his own, particularly with the move to acquire Skyways.

"The decision of Langton and Williams to sell out, allied to the entry of the International Thomson Organisation into leisure, was the end of an era, not of freedom exactly but of free rein for the airline. From a time of being terribly constrained through lack of cash, we now entered a new era and, though having lost some of the freedom of choice, we now had a cash-rich organisation behind us, particularly when North Sea oil came on stream. So we now had the ability to move ahead in a way most unlikely to have occurred had we not enjoyed the financial muscle associated with the takeover."

Derek Davison sometimes asks himself the question where the airline would have been today had it not been acquired by International Thomson.

"There have been opportunities open to Britannia Airways constrained by International Thomson. There are disciplines in being associated with a conglomerate, and they really do not allow some of the more daring and exciting moves which clearly have been there, are there at the moment, and could be there in the future. But without the cash and support from our parent, it is most unlikely Britannia would be the size it is today or have its first-class equipment. ITOL have been tremendously supportive, but we may have missed some of those exciting opportunities because we are part of a travel group and not an airline on its own."

If, in fact, that is so, Davison is certain it is not through any lack of imagination, initiative or purposeful endeavour by his own board of directors.

"With the change from isolated immediate decisions being the key to success in the early days to a host of decision-making events which became far more numerous as the company grew, there was a real need for a competent board working together as a team.

"I set out to achieve this and I was very fortunate in being able to do so in a fairly rapid timescale. In spite of premature losses from the board – the untimely and tragic loss of two technical directors, Geoff Parkins and Bill Buxton, in fairly quick succession – I believe it as strong today as ever.

"With our present balanced board we have a team of competent people who get on well together and make a host of good decisions separately and collectively. It is something for which I have striven right from the day I became chief executive. What is true of the board is equally true throughout Britannia with strong competent teams pulling in the same direction."

Though Jed Williams talked of what he called 'The Luton Formula' as being one of the original factors in the airline's initial success, because of the enthusiastic support of the airport operator, Derek Davison contemplates what might have been had the first choice of London Gatwick, as the airline's home base, been possible.

"Had we been at Gatwick then the Edwards report into the future of civil aviation in the UK might have come to a different conclusion about which should be the 'second force' airline in Britain alongside British Airways."

But the philosophy over the years since then has been, in Davison's words, to "pay single-minded attention" to the leisure market. That applies right to today – even their Ministry of Defence flights to Germany are leisure-oriented because many of the troops involved and their families are flying on leave.

An interesting change of emphasis can be noted in recent International Thomson Organisation external bulletins. Traditionally, these have referred to the organisation as "a leading international publishing and information business with strong interests in travel and oil and gas". But it is significant that the description has now been changed to "a leading publishing, information and leisure travel company with strong interests in oil and gas".

Davison suggests just one of many motives for the airline's attitude to leisure: "I think the business side of travel is getting less and less important. At one time it dominated the airplane market, then charter came along much of which was associated with leisure. Even then, business travel was still very important, but today it accounts for less than 20 per cent of the total European market by passengers.

"The growth everyone recognises is in the leisure market – the business market will grow in absolute terms, but in relative terms it is getting smaller and smaller. Anything that is worth having in the business market has already been taken. At very best, given a free-for-all in Europe through greater liberalisation, you would have to fight like hell for it against the big boys."

It is certain that liberalisation, through the moves towards deregulation of aviation in Europe, is something which must continue to exercise boardroom minds at Luton.

Derek Davison, who became a Commander of the Order of the British Empire in 1985, believes that what is now happening on the European scene is not totally dissimilar to what has been taking place in the United States.

"The majority recognise that deregulation has been good for the USA and that it has produced, in large measure, what it set out to produce – a huge decrease in cost for the average consumer. There are those who will argue that there has been a major reduction in safety standards, but that has not been the case. There may well have been some effect on safety. Such significant changes have side effects and demand responses. Those responses are and will be forthcoming.

"Nevertheless, even in the competitive environment of the USA, the small fry are being squeezed by the big boys – many things, including computer muscle, are making it very difficult for the little airlines to compete. With the major carriers in the public sector linked very solidly to national aspirations, together with historical, cultural and political factors, it is well nigh impossible to envisage deregulation in Europe on anything like the US scale. European style deregulation, however, is likely to present its challenges to the small privatised airlines.

"It worries me about getting first things first. The politicians are in such a hurry – they talk about lower costs to the public, and think that deregulating is the way of achieving that. There are no basic reasons for believing that would apply. In the United States it has happened through reductions in high wage levels which, through regulation, pushed salaries up out of all relation to other professional people doing responsible jobs where normal rules of competition did apply."

▲ *When the present Lord Thomson* (second left) *visited Luton in December 1985, he was entertained to lunch by the Britannia board. On his right is his son Peter, and from his left are Bob Parker-Eaton, Peter Brown, John Tory, deputy chairman of International Thomson Organisation, Dave Hopkins, Derek Davison, Brian Christian, Michael Brown, president of International Thomson Organisation, and Bernard Newton.*

Davison suggests that it would be wiser for politicians first to tackle Europe's high operating costs. He believes the way to reduce the cost of flying is, initially, to deal with the problems of its infrastructure, "but that is far less attractive to the politicians".

Looking at the longer term, Derek Davison believes that greater freedom of choice aided by growing discretionary income will sway the pattern of services being offered by Britannia.

"The 'de-packaging' of holidays will increase as the average member of the British public becomes more sophisticated in his requirements for both holidays and travel in general. As a consequence, I believe Britannia, in the future, will be dealing on a much bigger scale directly with the public who will develop a desire to travel further afield."

He thinks this process would already have happened if the massive fuel hike of the 1974 OPEC crisis had not occurred.

"When it does take place, the longer range aspects of our Boeing 767 fleet will come into play. There are two aspects to this. One is the desire simply for leisure in terms of sun, sand and sailing, though going further afield for it such as to the West Indies and North America, but the other important aspect is the cultural type of holiday. People wish to go and see the Great Wall of China, the tombs in Upper Egypt, or all the interesting places in the sub-continent of India, and so on. I think there will be developments in both these areas and that they will be significant. One will take people to the west and the other mainly to the east, but there will also be moves to the south. Africa is a very interesting continent – there is, for instance, already an appreciable amount of German tourism going to East Africa."

It is still, Derek Davison thinks, an open question on what role Britannia Airways, Thomson Holidays, or any other holiday company will play in this developing scene.

"We have a very good transportation system in Britannia, a very good marketing system, and a very good computer and data system to look after all these arrangements. But the question of whether these developments are carried out in the name of Britannia or a tour operator is not the issue. The real issue is that seats along these lines will be sold, and Britannia will fly to these destinations.''

In the foreseeable future this should provide corporate 'jam', whereas much bread-and-butter revenue will still come from the popular destinations, around the 1,000 mile sector routings, for which the 767 is ideal.

Derek Davison and his executives are now tackling the preliminaries to their next major fleet decision – the replacement in the coming decade of some of their inestimable aviation workhorses, the Boeing 737s.

Those assiduous aircraft manufacturing salesmen have already been making their presentations at Luton.

As Davison told his staff in 1986: ''There is a limit to the number of Boeing 767s relative to 737-sized aircraft which Britannia and its customers can support. Big aeroplanes are fine for high density routes, as the 767 has proved. To fill the seats of a large aircraft on lower density routes, however, frequency must be reduced compared to that which is possible when operating smaller aircraft. Therefore, we shall still need an aircraft of a capacity less than the 767.

''Our sights are on identifying the right aircraft to replace the 737. There is no hurry to do this – the 737 will be flying with Britannia well into the next decade. Providing we keep the 737 spick and span, both inside and out, it is unlikely to date in passenger terms. So we have time to consider the options open to us.''

Who, then, are the suitors presenting themselves at Britannia's court?

Though the next generation of the Boeing 737 – the 300 and 400 series – and McDonnell Douglas's DC 9-80/MD80 variants have specific attractions, they are not considered to provide, at present, the seat-mile costs Britannia would expect to have from its 737 replacement.

At one time, it appeared that a straight choice would be made between aircraft from the same two aeronautical camps who fought out the wide-bodied order at the beginning of the eighties – Boeing of the United States and Airbus Industrie of Europe.

Boeing has committed $5 billion to what it is calling its new technology aircraft, the 7J7. It is planned to be a 150-seater, but Chris Longridge, Boeing Commercial Airplane Company's vice president of marketing, says

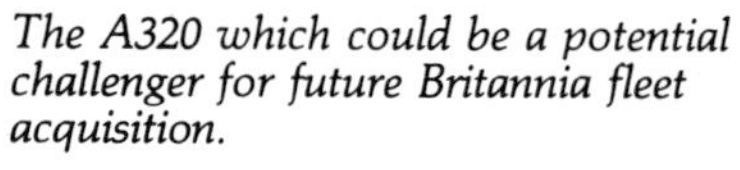

The A320 which could be a potential challenger for future Britannia fleet acquisition.

they would think, in inclusive tour configuration terms, of its seating from 170 to 175 passengers. Derek Davison would expect Britannia to make a contribution to the thinking on those high-density aspects. Projecting further ahead, they might well consider a smaller version, with a new cross section and smaller wings, which could equate with the present 130-seater 737s being operated by Britannia.

While the 7J7 was still a drawing-board aircraft, however, Airbus Industrie had already sold its A320, the smaller single aisle relative of the European Airbus. Following initial orders from Air France and British Caledonian, its biggest breakthrough was in its rival's heartland, when Northwest Airlines of Minneapolis signed in October, 1986, to buy 100 of the aircraft for $3.2 billion following an order a few months earlier from Pan American for both A320s and A310s.

Again, a critical factor which interested Northwest is that the A320 will fly 150 passengers at half the fuel consumed by its present short/medium haul fleet aircraft.

Both the 7J7 and the A320 have much new thinking in avionics, instrumentation and computer control.

But the choice is now not necessarily so clear cut because of the advent of what has become known as the 'unducted fan' engine. General Electric, Allison, Pratt & Whitney and Rolls-Royce are all working on this advanced propulsion technology.

Derek Davison believes now that it is well worthwhile waiting to see the outcome of this. "I think it is likely to be a success, otherwise these significant companies would not be spending the sort of money they are committing to it. I believe the only question mark is the timescale."

The point is that the unducted fan engine will offer a significant advantage in air transport costs for those aeroplanes fitted with it, even at present fuel prices, and the next few years may well see the advent of a plethora of aircraft using it, both new and existing types.

"It is going to be very interesting now in making our choice, but it is not going to be an easy decision," Davison suggests. He points out that the first jet engines moved small masses of air to the rear very rapidly, but the by-pass engines, of which the unducted fan philosophy is the latest example, move large masses of air back slowly. By-pass engines reduce the noise and improve the economics of the engine, but because

Another challenger, the projected Boeing 7J7 which has had $5 billion committed to its development, embracing much new technology.

The banners at the top of the page decorated the hangar when chairman Derek Davison held a special staff party in 1985 to congratulate them on achieving a million flying hours with the Boeing 737 fleet. In the photograph above he is addressing the 700 who attended the event.

the fan is free and not ducted in the new engine it is, at this stage, difficult to project the exact noise levels.

Derek Davison says it will be 1988, at the earliest, before they choose their 737 replacement. "We want to enjoy the benefits of time in our decision-making to improve the chances of getting it right."

However, he sees the immediate future for growth being against a background of an adequate mix in terms of the Boeing 737 and 767.

"We have an average age in the fleet of something like eight years and that is a pretty happy position. We are not paying, in spite of our new 767 fleet, enormous amounts of interest charges as we are getting the benefits from some of the older aircraft which have been written down. This provides a reasonably balanced position – if fuel prices go up significantly we are fairly well protected with the 767s, and if fuel goes down we are equally well protected with the older 737s."

He believes the airline is capable of absorbing more 767s to satisfy its growth in the next few years. But even if they were unable to absorb more 767s for any reason, then, assuming fuel prices do soar, they would be in a position to employ more 737 variants until they identify fleet replacement aircraft.

In the long term, he sees a return to the traditional pattern of advances in aviation where increase in speed was the criterion. The hurdle has been Mach 1 (645 miles an hour), but he believes that barrier will be overcome. The present different classes of accommodation in aircraft came about because airlines could not offer increased speed as an attraction. So growth in the size of aircraft allowed different levels of comfort.

"I believe we'll substantially get back to the position," says Derek Davison, "where speed is the main ingredient that the passenger is paying for. Therefore, comfort levels will tend to degrade and we'll see more aircraft like Concorde, where there is a degradation of comfort against the front areas of 747s, DC10s and TriStars, but people will be quite prepared

737 FLYING HOURS

to pay for it.

"We, in our business, will develop different classes in our aircraft to meet consumer demand. We have made a start, and I believe that will develop in future. Bear in mind, though, that we are in the leisure business and leisure is very price sensitive, paid out of discretionary income, and I don't see that changing for the next 100 years. Volume in our business is always going to be biased towards the same distances we have today.

"Supersonic leisure travel in our field? Possibly. We have assumed the economics of subsonic will always be superior to those of supersonic travel. But the essential of supersonic travel for a mass market is to find a method of propulsion which is different from today's fossil-based fuel. The amount of weight which has to be carried for the amount of thrust required is so high that present fuel is unlikely to produce reasonably priced supersonic travel. Whether it turns out to be rocket, nuclear or any other type of propulsion, we shall move into a different era, and it may then be quite wrong to assume that subsonic travel will be cheaper than supersonic any more.

"We have seen in the past where aeroplanes travelling faster and faster up to the present speeds have provided high increases in productivity. The aircraft flying at 600 miles an hour does approximately twice the work of an aircraft flying at 300 miles an hour and this advantage will always be there, albeit on a diminishing scale, particularly at shorter ranges."

Meanwhile, a man who had much to do with the evolution of those two present Britannia fleet aircraft is Joe Sutter, now retired from Boeing after earning the name 'Mr Jet' during his years as executive vice-president in charge of all their commercial aircraft engineering and new product development. He likes to tell the story of the day Britannia chairman Derek Davison undertook a trip he did not relish at all.

He had been visiting American engineering manufacturers General Electric and, with a couple of hours to spare afterwards, was persuaded to visit Disney World. Once there, he vehemently maintained he had no intention of taking one of the wild roller coaster rides on offer. However, Sutter's wife enticed him to try it, and to this day he regards it as one of his most forgettable 'flights'.

High and low points are, however, nothing new to Davison. They are endemic to the cyclical airline industry. Yet the determination and enthusiasm displayed by the Britannia Airways' team over the past 25 years have surely set the airline well on course for an impressive climb on its flightpath towards a fascinating second quarter century.

And Derek Davison confidently forecasts, given the same tremendous support of the past from the shareholders of the International Thomson Organisation, that, even by the end of the present century, Britannia Airways will be more than twice the size it had achieved at the end of its first 25 years. Still, as now, it will be dominantly a charter airline, but with a significantly increased proportion of its activity being by scheduled leisure services. By then, the prediction is that the present near ten million flying abroad for their inclusive holidays will have doubled to twenty million.

Even in his most visionary moments, Ted Langton could hardly have imagined that eventually passengers equalling in number more than a third of Britain's total population would become disciples of a holiday philosophy which all began with his simple, yet highly effective, 'hot-bed' routine.

▲

25 years' history in one picture. All four chief pilots of Britannia Airways are still serving in the airline in 1987 in various capacities. Bottom right is the current chief pilot Chris Norman and, clockwise from him, chairman Derek Davison, managing director Dave Hopkins, and operations director Stu Grieve.

THANK YOU FOR
FLYING BRITANNIA

HISTORY OF THE AIRLINE FLEET FROM 1962

1962

April
Delivery of first aircraft:
- G-ARVP Lockheed 049 Constellation (ex-El Al)
- G-AHEN Lockheed 049 Constellation (ex-El Al)
- G-ARXE Lockheed 149 Constellation (ex-El Al)

September
Negotiated agreement with receiver of Skyways to operate a number of aircraft on behalf of creditors:
- G-ALAL Lockheed 749C Constellation
- G-ALAK Lockheed 749C Constellation
- G-ANUR Lockheed 749C Constellation
- G-AHFB Avro York
- G-AGNV Avro York

Two aircraft ex-Trans-European Aviation:
- G-AHEL Lockheed 049 Constellation
- G-AMUP Lockheed 049 Constellation

1963

Summer fleet: eight Constellations, two Yorks.

Number of passengers carried: 67,512

1964

November: Bristol Britannia 102 (ex-BOAC) G-ANBB delivered.

Number of passengers carried: 131,296

1965

All Constellations were disposed of:
- G-ARVP broken up at Luton
- G-ARXE broken up at Luton
- G-AHEN broken up at Luton
- G-AMUP broken up at Luton
- G-ALAL sold to Ace Freighters
- G-ALAK sold to Ace Freighters
- G-ANUR sold to Ace Freighters
- G-AHEL sold to private operator
- York G-AHFB broken up at Luton
- York G-AGNV sold to Staverton Museum

January: Britannia 102 (ex-BOAC) G-ANBO delivered
February: Britannia 102 (ex-BOAC) G-ANBF delivered
March: Britannia 102 (ex-BOAC) G-ANBA delivered
July: Britannia 102 (ex-BOAC) G-ANBL delivered

Summer fleet: five Britannias

Number of passengers carried: 184,630

1966

February: Britannia 102 (ex-BOAC) G-ANBE delivered
March: Britannia 102 (ex-BOAC) G-ANBJ delivered
April: Britannia 102 (ex-BOAC) G-ANBI delivered
September: Britannia G-ANBB lost in an accident in Yugoslavia

Summer fleet: eight Britannias

Number of passengers carried 315,000

1967

Summer fleet: seven Britannias

Number of passengers carried: 326,802

1968

July: first 737-204 (G-AVRL Sir Ernest Shackleton) delivered
August: 737-204 (G-AVRM James Watt) delivered

Fleet size: seven Britannias; two 737s

Number of passengers carried: 463,200

1969

April: 737-204 (G-AVRN Captain James Cook) delivered
737-204 (G-AVRO Sir Francis Drake) delivered
May: 737-204 (G-AWSY General Sir James Wolfe) delivered

Summer fleet: five Britannias; five 737s

Number of passengers carried: 825,831

1970

January: 737 G-AVRL leased to Argentina 22.1.70 to 31.4.70
February: Britannia G-ANBI broken up at Luton
March: delivery of first cargo convertible 737-204C (G-AXNA Robert Clive of India)
April: second cargo 737-204C delivered (G-AXNB Charles Darwin, ex-City of Birmingham)
May: 737-204 delivered (G-AXNC Isambard Kingdom Brunel)
Britannia G-ANBF broken up at Luton
June: Britannia G-ANBA broken up at Luton

Fleet size: eight 737s

Number of passengers carried: 925,500

1971

February: leased Boeing 707-373C delivered G-AYSI
March: Britannia G-ANBJ broken up at Luton
May: Britannia G-ANBO broken up at Luton
Britannias G-ANBL and G-ANBE were also broken up at Luton in 1971
October: Boeing 707-355C delivered G-AYEX

Fleet size: eight 737s; two 707s

Number of passengers carried: 1,266,442

1972

February: 737-222 delivered (G-AZNZ Henry Hudson ex-City of Nottingham) ex-United Airlines

Fleet size: nine 737s; two 707s

Number of passengers carried: 1,616,103

1973

Two Boeing 707s disposed of to British Caledonian
January: 737-204 delivered (G-BADP Sir Arthur Whitten Brown) first advanced model.
March: 737-204 delivered (G-BADR Captain Robert Falcon Scott)
December: one 737 on Winter wet lease to Yemen Airways (G-AVRL) 12.12.73 to 19.6.74

Fleet size: eleven 737s

Number of passengers carried: 1,652,012

1974

January: 737-204 delivered (G-BAZG Florence Nightingale) first advanced with-15 engines
February: two 737-204s delivered (G-BAZH Sir Frederick Handley Page) (G-BAZI Sir Walter Raleigh)
June: G-AVRL returned from Yemen Airways 19.6.74. G-BAZG leased to Yemen 18.6.74 to 28.5.76
September: two 737s on Winter lease to Transavia Holland: G-AXNA 13.9.74 to 8.5.75; G-AVRN 1.12.74 to 25.3.75

Fleet size: fourteen 737s

Number of passengers carried: 1,850,000

1975

737s G-AXNA and G-AVRN returned from Transavia

Fleet size: fourteen 737s

Number of passengers carried: 2,000,000

1976

May: 737 G-BAZG returned from Yemen 28.5.76
November: 737 G-AVRO on lease to Far East Transport 26.11.76 to 16.4.77

Fleet size: fourteen 737s

Number of passengers carried: 2,267,527

1977

April: 737-219 delivered (G-BGNW George Stephenson) ex-Air New Zealand; 737-204 delivered (G-BECG Amy Johnson)
May: 737-204 delivered (G-BECH Viscount Montgomery of Alamein)
November: 737 G-AVRO on lease again to Far East Transport 1.11.77 to 26.4.78

Fleet size: seventeen 737s

Number of passengers carried: 2,407,040

1978

A 737-200 leased for summer from Transavia and another from Gulf Air (A40BG) for twelve months
November: two 737-204s delivered (G-BFVA Sir John Alcock) (G-BFVB Sir Thomas Sopwith)

Fleet size: nineteen 737s plus two leased

Number of passengers carried: 2,747,285

1979

Fleet size: nineteen 737s plus one leased

Number of passengers carried: 3,344,776

1980

January: two 737-204s delivered (G-BGYJ Sir Barnes Wallis) (G-BGYL Jean Batten) with increased max taxi weight from 117,500 lbs to 122,000 lbs.
February: 737-204 delivered (G-BGYK R. J. Mitchell)
April: 737-204 (G-BOSL Sir Frank Whittle) delivered and operated on behalf of O.S.L.
September: 737-204 delivered (G-BHWE Sir Sydney Camm)
December: 737-204 delivered (G-BHWF Lord Brabazon of Tara)

Fleet size: twenty-five 737s plus one on lease from Transavia

Number of passengers carried: 3,415,929

1981

May: second 737-244 (G-OSLA Sir Geoffrey de Havilland) delivered and operated on behalf of O.S.L.
November: 737 G-BGYJ on lease to Royal Brunei 15.11.81 to 19.12.81

Fleet size: twenty-six 737s plus one from Transavia and one from Eagle Air on lease

Number of passengers carried: 3,941,691

1982

April: two 737-204s delivered (G-BJCT The Hon. C. S. Rolls) (G-BJCU Sir Henry Royce)
May: 737-204 delivered (G-BJCV Viscount Trenchard)

Fleet size: twenty-nine 737s plus five leased 737-200s for summer (two Transavia, two Quebec Air, one Eagle Air)

Number of passengers carried: 4,156,607

1983

February: 737-204 delivered (G-BKHE Sir Francis Chichester)
March: 737-204 delivered (G-BKHF Alliott Verdon Roe)
October: G-OSLA (O.S.L. aircraft) disposed of to America West Airlines; G-BOSL disposed of to Dan Air

Fleet size: twenty-nine 737s

Number of passengers carried: 4,399,174

1984

February: first Boeing 767-204 delivered (G-BKVZ Sir Winston Churchill). Second 767-204 delivered (G-BKPW Earl Mountbatten of Burma)
October: 737 G-BGYJ leased to Midway Express until May 1985
November: 737 G-BJCU leased to Spantax (EC-DVE). Returned off lease November 30, 1985

Fleet size: twenty-nine 737s; two 767s

Number of passengers carried: 4,472,688

1985

February: third 767-204 delivered (G-BLKV)
March: fourth 767-204 delivered (G-BLKW Sir Frank Whittle)
April: 737s G-AZNZ and G-BAZI sold to Guinness Peat Aviation.
737 G-BHWE leased to British Airtours (Returned to Britannia April 1, 1987)
May: 737 G-BFVB leased to Nordair (C-GNDW). (Returned to Britannia April 30, 1986)
737 G-BJCT leased to Spantax (EC-DXK). (Returned to Britannia April 1, 1986)
737 G-BGYJ returned off lease from Midway Express
November: 737 G-BJCV leased to C.P. Air (C-GXCP). (Returned to Britannia April 28, 1986)
737 G-AVRM sold to Presidential Airlines (N312XV)

Fleet size: twenty-seven 737s; four 767s

Number of passengers carried: 4.3 million

1986

February: 737-2D6 leased from Air Mali TZ-ADL. Into service for Britannia April 1 (G-BMMZ)
April: 737 G-AVRL (first 737 delivery to Britannia in 1968) sold to Presidential Airlines (N311XV)
May: 737 G-AVRO sold to Presidential Airlines (N313XV)
737-247 leased from Air Belgium 00-PLH. Ended October 1986

Fleet size: four 767s; twenty-four 737s. Plus one leased from Air Mali and one from Air Belgium and one DC-8 from Canafrica.

Number of passengers carried: 5.55 million

1987

A fifth 767-204 G-BNCW joining the fleet on medium-term lease (until delivered, 767-205 G-BNAX operated on short-term lease ex-Varig)

Fleet size: five 767s; twenty-four 737s, plus one 737-2D6 leased from Air Mali, one 737-2E1 from Aer Lingus, one 737-2A3 from Transavia (ex-Pluna, Uruguay) and one 737-2T5 from Guinness Peat Aviation (ex-Orion).

1988

Spring: A new 767-204 will be delivered bringing the airline's wide-bodied fleet to six.

TECHNICAL DETAILS OF MAIN FLEET AIRCRAFT FROM 1962

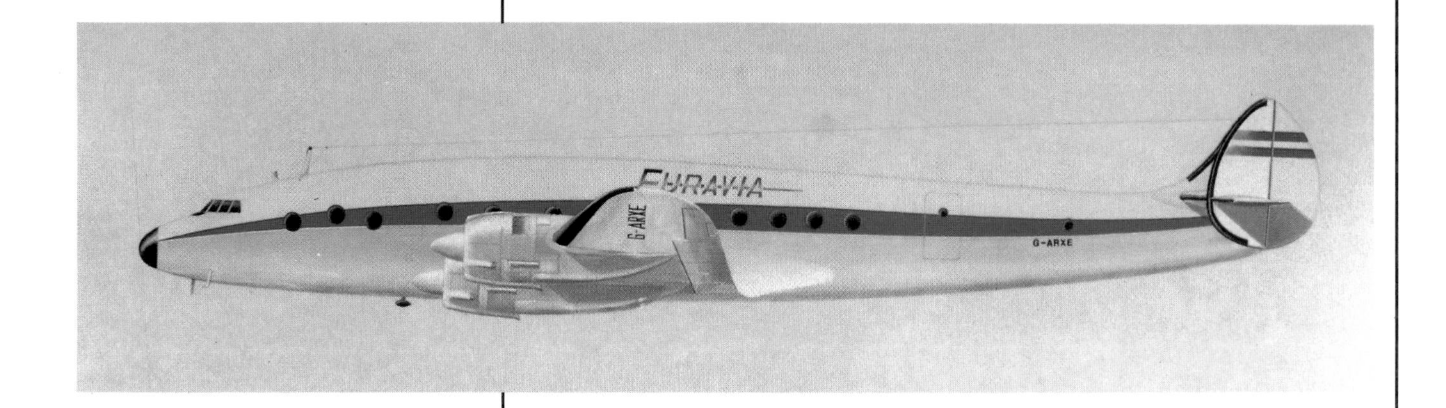

CONSTELLATION 049 and 149

Powered by 4 Wright Cyclone BA3 power plants (2200 HP)
18 cylinder radial – 2 rows of 9.
3 bladed V.P. hydromatic propeller. 15ft 2in diameter.

CONSTELLATION 749

Powered by 4 Wright Cyclone BD1 power plants (2500 HP)
18 cylinder radial – 2 rows of 9.
3 bladed "Curtis" V.P. electric propeller

CONSTELLATION – General

Fully pressurised, capacity 82 passengers
Cruise altitude 19,000ft
Range 2,610 nautical miles to a maximum of 4,785 nautical miles
Wing span – 123ft
Length – 95ft 1¼in
Maximum weight – 107,000 lbs
Cruise speed 260/290 m.p.h.

AVRO YORK

Powered by 4 Rolls Royce Merlin 20's 500 series (rated at 1,620 H.P.) V12
Engines water cooled (Ethylene Glycol)
3 bladed de Havilland constant speed propeller, controlled by a C.S.U.
Fuel consumption – 50 gallons per engine per hour in cruise

YORK – General

Up to 60 passengers but used mostly for freight
Aircraft unpressurised
Cruising altitude 10,000ft; max service ceiling 23,000ft.
Range with max payload 1,200 nautical miles
Wing span – 102ft
Length – 78ft 6ins
Maximum weight – 70,000 lbs
Maximum cruise speed 260 m.p.h.

BRISTOL BRITANNIA 102

Powered by 4 Bristol Proteus 705 turbo-props (3,780 E.H.P. each engine)
Free turbine-propeller connected by shaft direct to turbine (via reduction gear)
Propeller – de Havilland 4 bladed steel or dural prop.
Hydro-electric (16ft diameter)

BRITANNIA 102 – General

Capacity – 117 passengers
Wing span – 142ft 3½in
Length – 114ft
Height – 36ft 8in
Maximum take-off weight – 155,000 lbs
Cruising speed 375 m.p.h.
Still air range with 25,000 lbs load is 3,385 nautical miles; with 14,000 lbs load, 4,617 nautical miles
Fuel tanks consisted of 9 rubber cells in each wing (bag tanks) total cap. – 6,690 gallons
Aircraft fully pressurised
Cruise altitude 19,000 – 22,000 ft

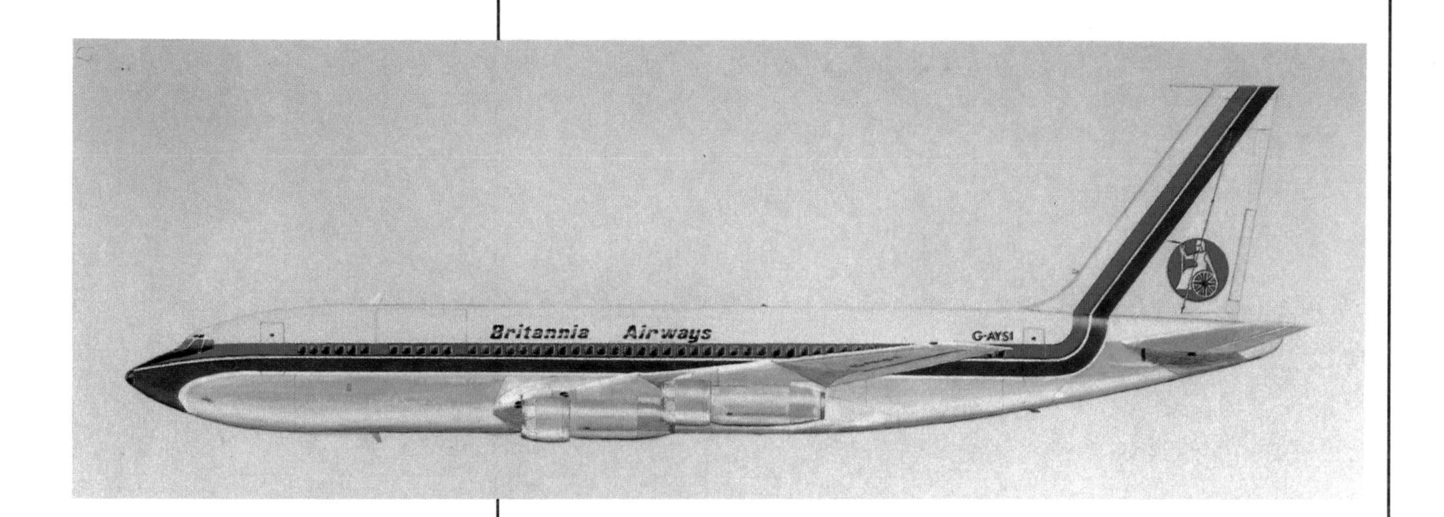

BOEING 707-320C

Powered by 4 Pratt & Whitney JT3D-3B turbofans rated at 18,000 lbs thrust
Seating – 6 abreast, single aisle, 189 configuration
Cargo configuration – 79,400 lbs cargo
dimensions – Wing span 145ft 9 in
Length 145ft 6 in
Height 42ft 6in
Cruising speed – 575 m.p.h.
Mach number – 0.90M (25,000ft and above)
Maximum range – 6,000 nautical miles
Maximum cruising altitude – 42,000ft

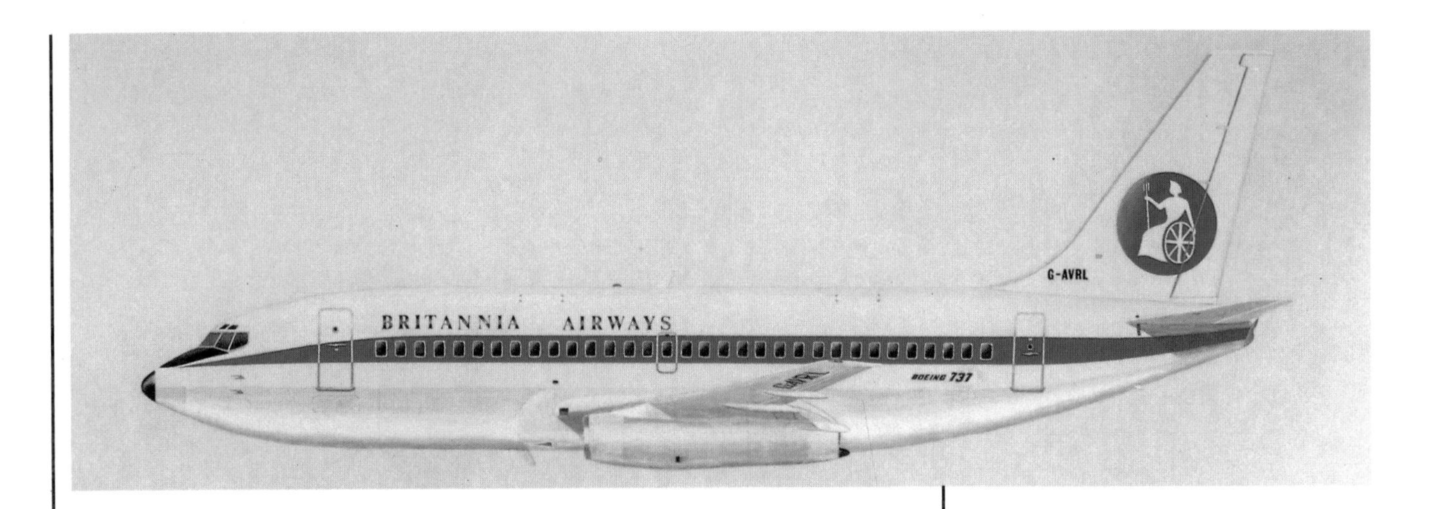

BOEING 737-200

Powered by 2 Pratt & Whitney JT8D-9 or -15 turbo fans rated at 14,500 lbs (-9) or,15,500 lbs (-15) thrust each
Seating – 6 abreast, single aisle, 130 configuration
Dimensions: Wing span 93ft
Length 100ft 4in
Height 37ft
Maximum take-off weight 117,000 lbs (JT8D-9) or 121,500 lbs (JT8D-15)
Maximum range – 1,650 nautical miles (JD8D-9) or, 1,854 nautical miles (JT8D-15)
Cruising speed – 490 m.p.h.
Maximum cruising altitude – 37,000ft

BOEING 767-200

Powered by 2 CF6-80A rated at 48,000 lbs thrust each (General Electric)
Seating – 8 abreast, twin aisle – 2-4-2. 273 configuration
Dimensions – Wing span 156ft 1in
Length 159ft 2in
Height 52ft
Maximum take-off weight up to 345,000 lbs.
Cruising speed – 540 m.p.h.
Mach. number 0.80 M (39,000ft)
Maximum cruising altitude – 43,000ft
Maximum range with payload – up to 4,400 nautical miles

All this fleet information was compiled by Barry Crossland, Britannia Airways' component control superintendent, who, as a schoolboy, saw the first Constellation aircraft bought by the airline arrive at Luton Airport.

Britannia
BOEING 767

Index

An italic figure indicates an illustration